INSIDE THE STRETCH OF MY HEART

Also by Susan Noble

Before and After the Darkness
Drifting Between Empty Tramlines
Collected Poems
The Dream of Stairs: A Poem Cycle
A Flock of Blackbirds

INSIDE THE STRETCH OF MY HEART

Poems from Morning to Night

Susan Noble

AESOP Poets
Oxford

AESOP Poets
An imprint of AESOP Publications
Martin Noble Editorial / AESOP
28 Abberbury Road, Oxford OX4 4ES, UK
www.aesopbooks.com

First paperback edition published by AESOP Publications
Copyright (c) 2014 The Estate of Susan Noble

The right of the Estate of Susan Noble to be
identified as the author of this work has been
asserted in accordance with sections 77 and 78
of the Copyright Designs and Patents Act 1988.
A catalogue record of this book is available
from the British Library.

Condition of sale:
This book is sold subject to the condition that it shall not, by way of
trade or otherwise, be lent, sold or hired out or otherwise circulated in
any form of binding or cover other than that in which it is published
and without a similar condition including this condition being
imposed on the subsequent purchaser.

ISBN: 978-1-910301-03-6

Contents

Preface		xiii
Publisher's note		xv
PART I	MORNING	21
1	Day	23
2	Journey	24
3	Call	25
4	Time	26
5	Waking	27
6	Morning	28
7	Monday Morning	29
8	When Morning Is Whiter than Shell	30
9	Aversion	31
10	Tube-Time	32
11	Nine to Five-Thirty	33
12	The Bureaucrat	34
13	Sartoris	36
14	Intercom	37
15	Through the Barrier	38
16	Paper Children	39
17	Chain	40
18	Communication in Silence	41
19	Dust	42
20	Launderette	43
21	Morning Break	44
22	Telephone	45
23	Crossed Line	46
24	Moment	47
25	The Reading	48

26	*The Bluffer*	49
27	*Worms*	50
28	*Portent*	51
29	*Incommunicado*	52
30	*Torpor*	53

PART II   MIDDAY   55

31	*Living-Room*	57
32	*Ugliness*	58
33	*The Boast*	59
34	*Fishes*	60
35	*Summer*	61
36	*Bubble*	62
37	*Lunchtime*	63
38	*Crowd*	65
39	*The Blind Man*	67
40	*Off Peak*	68
41	*The Joke*	69
42	*The Bore*	70
43	*Kibbutz*	71
44	*Vacuum*	72
45	*Trafalgar*	73
46	*Outsize*	74
47	*The Enemy*	75

PART III   AFTERNOON   77

48	*A Flock of Blackbirds*	79
49	*Dragons' Teeth*	80
50	*Street Dance*	81
51	*Stifled*	82
52	*Friday Afternoons*	83

53	*Interruption*	84
54	*Bank Holiday*	85
55	*Park-Time*	86
56	*Rainy Day in the Tourist Season*	87
57	*Misunderstanding*	88
58	*Shadows*	89
59	*Pity*	90
60	*Bones*	91
61	*Meeting*	92
62	*Fishing*	93
63	*Time Machine*	94
64	*Boredom*	95
65	*Teatime*	96
66	*On the Steps*	97
67	*Museum Piece*	98
68	*Silk-Worm*	99
69	*Growth*	100
70	*Downpour*	101
71	*Lost Between Stone Basins*	102
72	*Age*	103
73	*Those Who Do Not Question Much*	104
74	*Ephraim*	105
75	*Malaise*	106
76	*Verdure*	107
77	*Parasite*	108
78	*Double Biology*	109
79	*Old Woman*	110
80	*Lemon*	111
81	*To Forestall*	112
82	*Acorn*	113
83	*Saturday Afternoon*	114
84	*Bus*	115
85	*Hunger*	117
86	*Food-Time*	118

87	*The Waiter*	119
88	*The Waitress*	120
89	*Cactus*	121
90	*View*	122
91	*Pier*	123
92	*Six o'clock*	124
93	*Flight*	125
94	*The Stones*	126

PART IV　EVENING　127

95	*Label*	129
96	*Summer Evening*	130
97	*Tube*	131
98	*Image*	132
99	*The Evening Class*	133
100	*Routine*	134
101	*No Danger*	135
102	*Rosanna*	136
103	*Foretaste*	137
104	*Trendy People*	138
105	*Hypnosis*	139
106	*Bio-energetics*	140
107	*Last Respects*	141
108	*Shyness*	142
109	*Interior*	143
110	*Stepping Outside*	144
111	*Surprise*	145

PART V　NIGHT　147

112	*Night*	149
113	*Loss*	150
114	*Winter*	151

115	Midnight at the Station	152
116	Platform	153
117	The Fainting	154
118	Party Time	155
119	Party Games	156
120	Dream of Oxford	158
121	Christmas Eve	159
122	Reality	160

PART VI   INDOORS   161

123	Yoga	163
124	Mouse	164
125	Insect	165
126	Television	166
127	Reminder	167
128	Passive Involvement	168
129	The Deaf Ear	169
130	The Search	170
131	Why Write?	171
132	The Poet	172
133	To Write	173
134	Writing	174

PART VII   THE TEN DAYS OF PENITENCE   175

135	The Ten Days of Penitence	177
136	Memory	178
137	Egg	179
138	Roaming	180
139	Filter	181
140	Brain	182
141	Jealousy	183

CONTENTS

142	*Distrust*	184
143	*The Scapegoat's Cry*	185
144	*The Choice*	186
145	*Display*	187
146	*Questions and Answers*	188
147	*The Will*	189
148	*Instant*	190
149	*God and Satan*	191
150	*Psychology*	192
151	*Sanity*	193
152	*The Future*	194
153	*Evil*	195
154	*Turbulence*	196
155	*Façade*	197
156	*Current of Belief*	198
157	*Double Glazing*	199
158	*The Line of Memory*	200
159	*Over-Exposure*	201
160	*Rat-Race*	203
161	*Reflector*	204
162	*Tightrope*	205
163	*Eyes*	206
164	*Success*	207
165	*Oyster*	208
166	*The Smile*	209
167	*Needlepoint*	210
168	*Four-Leaved*	211
169	*Two Cures*	212
170	*Two Sides*	213
171	*Involvement*	214
172	*Divorce*	215
173	*Widow Spider*	216
174	*Sophistication*	217

CONTENTS

175	Photo	218
176	Fifty Per Cent	219
177	No Resting Place	220
178	Infection	221
179	Wasted Years	222
180	Acquiescence	223
181	Frost	224
182	Meditating	225
183	Six Haikus	226
184	Respect for the Elders	227
185	Snowdrop	228
186	The Ascetic	229
187	War Baby	230
188	Occupational Therapy	231
189	Camera	232
190	Sacrifice	233
191	Fallen Away	234
192	Song of the Crow	235
193	We Follow Our Gods	236
194	Fire	237
195	Tulip	238
196	Smiled upon a Face	239
197	Cycle	240
198	Sun on the Track	244
199	No Further Can I Go	245
200	Wallflower	246
201	Peace	247

Index of Poems	249
Index of First Lines	255

xi

Preface

About the book

Inside the Stretch of My Heart, subtitled *Poems from Morning to Night*, traces the perceptions of a poet through the course of a single day. These poems are triggered by the quotidian experience of living and working in central London in the late 1960s and early 1970s, yet beneath the fragile surface of Susan Noble's acute observations of domestic and office life in the city, intensely spiritual insights are being played out, sometimes delicately, sometimes shockingly, but always movingly.

This volume is a companion collection to *The Dream of Stairs: A Poem Cycle*, which was privately printed as a posthumous memorial volume in 1975, a year after my sister Susan's untimely death in 1974 at the age of 31. Susan wrote the poems in batches of half a dozen or more, from 1965 onwards, in what she described as manic bursts of creativity, announcing with her typically light-hearted ironic self-depreciation, 'The muse has struck me!' But these poems are anything but light-hearted, and even a first reading will reveal clearly that levity is not on the menu in a universe 'Where there are no jokes / And people do not pretend.'

Susan Noble's output in the final ten years of her life was prolific and to mark the fortieth anniversary of her death, the poems in this present collection have been published for the first time, together with a revised, expanded edition of *The Dream of Stairs*, a further collection, *Before and After the Darkness*, along with *Collected Poems*, containing all three poetry collections.

In addition, two volumes of Susan's fiction are being published: *A Flock of Blackbirds* (selected short stories and novellas) and the novel *Drifting Between Empty Tramlines*.

Profits from the sales of all six volumes are being donated to three charities: Mind, the Samaritans and Sane. For more details, see page xv. Facsimiles of the original typescripts and manuscripts are available online at:

www.aesopbooks.com/susannoble

Martin Noble
Oxford, 2014

PREFACE

About the author

Brought up in South London, my sister, Susan Noble, was the second of three children. Her childhood was enriched by being part of our large and closely-knit Jewish family. Unfortunately stricken by polio (then known as infantile paralysis) in her early years, Susan went through life with a degree of physical handicap which she was to overcome with courage and determination.

Educated at Croydon High School, Susan studied English at Somerville College, Oxford. After graduating, Susan worked in London, first at the Royal National Institute for the Blind, dictating books for transcription into Braille, and later at the National Central Library in London, where she qualified as a Chartered Librarian.

Susan's exceptional sensitivity was reflected in the prolific outpouring of poems that make up *Inside the Stretch of My Heart*, *The Dream of Stairs* and *Before and After the Darkness*. In these intense, haunting poems, she chronicles her personal response to the world around her, while vividly portraying the inner landscape of her mental and emotional struggle.

Judith Frankel
Netanya, 2014

Susan Noble

One's first impression of Susan was of fragility. She was an acutely sensitive person, but her physical and emotional fragility really masked a very great spiritual strength.

Her sensitivity indeed was not directed only towards herself, but towards others. She was sensitive to the needs of others, and her strength and also perhaps some of her inner conflicts came from a deep desire for goodness which could not be matched in reality by the world as she found it.

Susan passionately wished to be independent; she struggled for it from the time she went to university, and throughout her work as a librarian, and she was able to maintain it to the very end.

There was an intellectual and emotional intensity which burned within her and which predominantly found outward expression in her writing and when she expressed herself thus she did so with great imaginative power and also with an uncompromising honesty and integrity.

The late Rabbi Dr David Goldstein
South London, July 1974

Publisher's note

All profits from the sale of this volume
are being donated to the following charities:

The National Association for Mental Health
www.mind.org.uk

www.samaritans.org

www.sane.org.uk

Inside the Stretch of My Heart

I felt a circle of ears beyond the trees,
A stillness over the olive flower-beds
And I knew in that second
That I was one person,
Locked up inside a bag of pink skin,
Inside the stretch of my heart,
That all the love I had ever felt
Was rolling away down the hillside,
A crowd of shadow-figures from the past
Were toppling away for ever

from *Loss*

PART I

MORNING

1   *Day*

The earth turns rebel against itself
Green satin falls away from the root
The caterpillar tugs off its horny membrane
To the rhythm of the earth-beat,
Pulse of larva cycle
Acorn shells fall away
Each action dislodges the next
Until the course of events
Is pressed together in a concertina hold
And then released
Waves of sound
Like crushed glass
Rolling into the sea.

2 *Journey*

Endless book of days,
Each night follows with pictures of day,
Snatched away
Into truthful distortion.
I read this life
Stretching the muscle of mind
Into new places.
A diamond with many facets
Could not cut as sharply
As these sights overlap
Yet cannot be valued.
Redefined,
I see a clear track.
Train sweeps down the line,
Yet cannot believe that never
Will the journey be perfected;
Can only be read,
A page of days shows sometimes
A good sequence,
But today will be a slippery journey.

3   *Call*

Some eagle hovers overhead
It presages a message.
Steals something away.
Is it my conscience
Beating aside the evil,
Off, away;
Or perhaps a ghost from an old era
When things were wholesome
And fitted into place,
Calling me back,
Back and away,
Back
Back and through?

4 *Time*

Mother breaks through
The barriers
Into the born child.
Mirror cracks the night in two.
Future
Carries down seeds,
To join the first day to the last.
Who knows the past exactly?
Lost,
It comes out sometimes,
In a glance of déjà vu,
Hovers between the lips of clairvoyant speakers,
Surprised by its own power.
No ghost reversing back from the future
Can rattle and groan
To tell of the changes that will come to pass;
They cannot be caught by he shocking speed of light.
Baby smells of warm milk
And wobbles its head.
The broken cords between mother and birth
Jerk back
Into identification.

5   Waking

Force open these eyelids shuttered so tightly,
The cinema-screen of a nonsense dream-world.
The morning breezes enter so lightly,
Relieving the dusk of gloom that nightly
Descends on us from the sky uncurled.

Softly adapt yourself to the dawnday,
Shadows of sleep drift over the ceiling,
Where genuine flickers with dream-echoes play
In harmony round every jubilant sunray.
The grey depth of sleep is salted away
By the pure, purging slap of morning's cool sting.

6 *Morning*

Scorching light of day.
White fire
Falls, in a curtain
Onto the streets of London,
Rubs away the shadows and the flame
Of yesterday,
When twilight
Hung heavy as mould
Between the crevices,
Like grass growing in heaps,
Cannot be weeded out.
Now,
Bath of light
Purges
Into bone
The city centre.
Skeleton of ivory
Cannot weep,
Bare-eyes stare
At its nudity.

7 *Monday Morning*

Leap into the white void of Monday morning.
Fill it up with gestures, words,
A layer of grey shingle at the base of a tubular glass,
Craggy stones to bear the weight
Of the diminishing week,
Until the apex of Saturday
Crumbled off into Sunday
And slithers down to the bottom of the funnel once again.

8 *When Morning Is Whiter than Shell*

When morning is whiter than shell
And many moments part towards pain
And hasten to peace
Then do I know
The true mirror
Of myself.

9 *Aversion*

The cat, a seething kettle,
Paws and claws at my clothes,
Bounces back at every push
And curves around the mahogany table legs
Like melted plaster
Head points into the air to take a bite of oxygen
And lifts a bent paw as if wounded,
But I have no sympathy
The persistence of the intrusion
Negates the docility behind the gurgling purr
And I surprise myself by my aversion
To this patch of furry flesh,
That only wishes to communicate.

10 Tube-Time

In the tube
At twenty minutes to nine,
There is no space to breathe.
Only a hedge of bodies, Worzel Gummidges in coats.
Lost in a world of red angora and grey-flecked tweed
I sink back into the past
And fall forward into the end-of-tunnel future,
After the jolting to find a soft destination.
There is no time or space within this place,
No name for it.
Only the chugging along the tunnel
And the stations on either side
Are chopped off, snippeted away
Leaving a clean-cut circle of human cushions.

11 *Nine to Five-Thirty*

Daily routine of
Coil upon coil of workdays,
Springing up, never ending;
Trapping you with tight wire rings,
Which bruise the arms, disallow gymnastics.
Only the bobbing dance of the donkey tied to a stake,
Which mesmerises him into acceptance.

12 *The Bureaucrat*

Circle
Shoes in the morning
Sun white through the gate past the houses up for auction
Train　　　　　　　　desk　　　　　　　　papers
Three biros　　　　　　one black　　two red
And a pencil going blunt,
Grey flint bulge
Stone eyes of the watchful workers
Locked off into their weekday portholes
Sinking in the afternoon
As the sun snaps into
Six o'clock
Slowly
Very old dust
Train　　　　　　　　newspaper　　　　barricade
Through gate
Wash the feet
In soap orange-tan smelling of leather and thyme
Cleansed
No traces　　　　　　　into evening　　and fall over
The night
The bed lurches with the
Clock bell
Sun　　　　　cold　　　　　　white　　　hostile
Through the gate past the houses up for auction
Smell orange leather and tan and
Some spice

Cannot tell
Catch a new face perhaps a slice of news today
Eyes blue as slate
Hot watchful locked in portholes
Submarine nearing land

A square woman
In a tweed suit, brown checks upon the pink
Nothing achieved in her past sixty years
But the weekly paypacket and a long, long line
Of downtrodden subordinates
Having successfully held them under the water
And lashed out at her enemies, her peers
She can now surface to the water's top
With a spiral of bubbles
Lungs unused to the open air, gasping angrily
A lifetime of labour
Energy driven out in all directions
Only to find a long white sky
Upon an empty ocean

13   *Sartoris*

Birds   singing silver
Outside   rain-splashed ground
Inside   office
Papers   files
I wish   I wish   I wish   I wish
For ever
Birds   singing silver
Above the rain-splashed ground

14 *Intercom*

The pigeon coos mercilessly
Outside the office
Pleading for some love
Or turning instead to hypnosis
By repeated strain of winged throat
Inside the concrete and glass
Heads buzz, training
Figures into data
Coil upon coil
Torment and change

15 Through the Barrier

No moment will ever be more real than this one.
It is not before,
It is not after.
Morning coffee in the office
Cannot break out of the routine,
Wrench away the bars.
There will never be any walking through
Into a more vital area of emerald fields
And shimmering air,
Tiny yellow flowers that smell of wine,
And eyes that explain all in a pinpoint.
The shadows on the dusty typewriter
Hide the other side
Of living,
That cannot be pierced.
The girl by the window looks out and sighs.
The slink of a spoon against china
Overlaps onto her reality.
Yellow and blue turn to green.
She throws the past and the future
Onto a carpet of black velvet,
Packages wrapped in fancy paper and red ribbon bows
Tumble onto the ripples of gleaming pile.
She is sucked through a funnel of black velvet
Into the pinpoints of dust.
This second is this second.

16 *Paper Children*

Invisible strings
Sweep the squares and corrugated cuttings
Of paper along the pavement.
A yellow tube-ticket flies up in the air
In a trilling spiral
And flickers down again,
Beaten to the ground by the age old
Dominating parent of gravity.

Paper children – green shield stamps and pink receipts,
Blue tissue paper and red chocolate wrappers
Rise up to beat the air in adolescent rebellion.
Only one buff envelope manages to float away,
Down the pavement and round the corner,
Where it is stamped to shreds by a can-kicking
Teenager not recognising
His own reflection in the footmarks.
He mangles it with a screw of the heel
And hurries down the road towards the music shop.

17 *Chain*

Bonds that break and merge
Day in, day out,
The fibres interlinking.
Six workers in an office bound together
By liking, rivalry, civility.
A quarrel. Two threads snap.
A promotion. One more.
Fatigue. Two more.
Only one thread tenuously remains to provide
The nucleus for the renewing
In waves,
Flux
Of bondage
That will re-emerge and unite them all once again.

18 *Communication in Silence*

For four years we have worked in the same building,
A large place,
Often silence.
You superior to me in rank by far,
We have exchanged perhaps ten sentences
Over the past four years
And yet I know you.
I do not know your house, your friends, your family,
Only your stillness.
Quiet thought,
Efficiency.
Yet not mechanical,
Springs from a pious fervour,
The wish to justify daily bread,
Or the belief in the value of effort.
If I stay here for another four years
Or even eight,
We may perhaps exchange another ten sentences,
Or even twenty,
Yet I will never know you any the better.

19 *Dust*

Strange to see this familiar face,
Nothing new,
Old white speckles in the air,
Dust from morning sleep at the ebb of the week,
Silence and dust.
Same voice pulls out
Remembered pictures of summer afternoons.
Growing old in the dust;
The grey steel ebb of another moment
Falling into the next.

20 *Launderette*

The washing-machine's stomach
Is in pain,
Heaves around with clothes.
The people seated on benches at different angles
Of impatience
Listen to the hum and vibration
In anticipation.
They will be here at the same time
Next Sunday morning,
Eagerly awaiting a new birth.

21 *Morning Break*

A typewriter tapping, dust upon my desk
In the shape of an L,
An empty stomach,
Dry itchy skin
From oversleeping.
Reluctantly at work
Out of the office into a pool of lemon sunlight
Filtered through green leaves
In a latchwork. Not computerised
Or mechanised,
But rambling, intricate.
I fetch a carton of milk from the dairy.
The street is dotted with people
Bubbling and laughing.
I stand on the pavement,
Guilt at hunger winning
The conflict of the body and the mind.
I gulp the cold air and pay the penalty,
Thin lashes of sunlight.

22 *Telephone*

The telephone.
Black furry ear
Closes
Into slot,
Black pool of total immersion,
Overlapping vibrations,
That play a tissue tune.
Somewhere
Over the wires,
Between the poles along the tracks.
Stops the voice to gasp
And lose itself against the white metal
Of overhanging sky.
Wind slips across;
A blackbird hovers
And forgets to sing,
Flapping
Wayward confusion.
Here
Lies only
Communication.

23   Crossed Line

Listening to two conversations at once,
I gave the wrong answer to each,
Smiled briskly at the weeping girl by my shoulder
And uttered words of sympathy
To the business-caller at the other end
Of the black receiver.
So it is each day
Our minds
Cannot make a note on the jotter for the right call,
Cannot respond to the millions upon millions,
I do not exaggerate,
Of winking eyes and flashes of light around us,
Crossed line.
I can only apologise for this galaxy of confusion.

24   *Moment*

At this moment,
I have curved round the legs of the chair,
And jumped into the Wedgwood mug,
Disintegrated between the jumping
Letters of the newspaper,
Hang in the fuzzy air
And drill outside the window with the crane.
I see the sleeping cows in Dorset
And the apples in the greengrocer's shop
Across the road,
I lie breathing inside my lungs,
Waiting for the ribcage to swell out once more
And topple over into the next contraction.

25 *The Reading*

Hair aflame with the heat,
Eyes gummed up with the sunlight,
Hand dropping over the musty books,
Want to sleep,
Slee-ee-p.
Slowly
Prodded awake by the spiky rows of words,
Black conglomerations of tiny hieroglyphics,
Pretending to be phrases and meanings,
But actually mere pressings of black ink
Against mashed white wood-pulp.
Drop the pretence and
Slee-ee-p.

26 *The Bluffer*

We were talking in a hut on a strange Israeli morning,
The sabra-boy and me
And I regretted to myself
His lack of education, formally I mean,
For his schooling had been little
But by nature so much was there in him
He said that laughing children
Were like stars falling askew from the sky
And I in admiration
Thought everything he spoke was original,
If not profound,
Or so it seemed,
For he had picked it up from those around him,
His phrases and conceptions were copied,
Not self-begotten,
Acquired from men
Whom afterwards I met myself
And then I recognised the source
And they rang hollow.
Why did it matter? Words are words, ideas ideas,
Even though churned out by a second receiver,
And I'm sure the spark of originality was there
In my deceiver, only not so much as I had thought,
It was just a question of degree!

27 *Worms*

When I was young and the rain poured down,
The pavements were cluttered with silky pink worms
That lay straddled in sophisticated coils of contortion
Like weary corpses, except that they were both alive
And also resilient to the splitting stab,
Which instead of annihilating them,
Merely increased their life-force by two hundred per cent.
Today I never notice them, alive, split or otherwise
Perhaps I am not perceptive any more,
Or perhaps growing weary
Of their continual fight for survival
They creep into cracks in the pavement as I go by
And wait for me to overtake them
Before they loop their way out into the open air again
With assumed nonchalance.

28 *Portent*

Over the morning hangs
Third eye,
Cyclops second sight,
Plumply in the middle like a grape
Of bulbous ice.
I will go through.
The night will write a different script
From the printed message of yesterday.
It will mirror bluntly.
Glazed spears of angular disturbance
Will shoot once more
Their gunpowder anger.

Cloud of the afternoon
Grey as an old potato lump
Hangs slantingly;
Portends all that could arise
Unexpected looking-glass
Black shapes march across in flailing rhythm
Strange the directions
Which they can take
Away to the unaccountable places
Only to stay,
Black box of self, packed light as a cube of soiled ice
And never to meet.

29 *Incommunicado*

Three words.
Brief answer to his torrent of affection.
Pursed lips, once red,
Now almost grey in the ten o'clock light
Of Saturday morning.
Cups upon the draining-board are brown
With the stains of old tea.
The waters clings tepidly to her fingers.
Her age now apparent to him. He speaks again,
His arm curved round the edge of the kitchen steps,
Expansive, hopeful.
Three words.
Brief answer. He droops.

30 *Torpor*

In the antique shop on the corner,
The bald head of the shopkeeper
Is bent over a rail of old rugs,
Red and ginger flowers, threadbare greens,
And the cream ear upside down does not hear
The tinkle of the door, as I enter.
A jingle of light music is jogging up and down,
Vibrating the three vases on the window-sill,
Yellow, blue and green.
I spear the frozen shell of glass with an invisible finger
Racing impatience, as people walk by outside the window
And I am trapped by the lockjaw crouch
Of the silent old man;
But slowly, infected by his torpor I dissolve
And fall to rest inside the blue cave-bowl
Of the vase in the middle,
Particles of sea and sky.

PART II

MIDDAY

31 *Living-Room*

Blue cushions,
Plumped out,
Smug,
As duck's breasts
Upon the carpet.
I will not be deceived
By the midday sunlight,
That transforms the living-room
Into lemon stillness.
The sea is grey and salty,
When it flicks lashes
Of mud into dead fish.
This dry room,
Heated,
Painted hangings,
Is not here.
It is a slowly built makepiece
To hide
The sky of ice
And wet twilights,
Which really sting.

32 *Ugliness*

We met on a blistering summer's noonday
On a bench in the glare of a sweltering park.
I was afraid of him, he was a stranger
And also he happened to be rather ugly.
I had to sit near him for lack of space
And I was afraid of his unpleasant face
So strong is the force of conventional attitude
But he chatted away with agreeable platitude
So that his aura of strangeness departed
And I became friendly and almost warm-hearted
And his gleaming white teeth also reassured me,
They were part of the benevolent forces that be.
The very next week I met him in town,
Out of the blue and quite unexpectedly,
He, unaware of me, wore a bleak frown
And I was revolted all over again,
Though I tried not to be, not to be, not to be.
Then once again he revealed a white grin
And my world was restored to focus again
To its old satisfactory congruity.

33 *The Boast*

The boast
Spilled out of my lips
In the hot sunlight.
Bubbled with energy
And ten surprised eyes
Stared back at me,
Small black points against pale cheeks.
I wanted to pull the sentence back,
Like a yoyo on a cord.
But it was too late.
The thoughts had grown and burst like a soap bubble
Flat against the grained wood of the desk,
Its seeds now distasteful
Like the scum of old soap.

34 *Fishes*

Sitting at twin tables
I see
Your white seamed lips, twin fishes, smiling
Surprisingly,
Where I did not expect it.
Your table, a solid block of brown wood,
Has frizzled to gold in the sun
And midday has dazzled a shoal of painted fishes
Over my head.
I am lightbound and unstrung.
We are twin people.
Why then do you curve into a smile,
When all I can feel inside the golden net of my head
Is blackness?
You are the pain inside my hollow head,
The mud, where the golden fishes used to swim.
Why then do you smile, white seamed lips,
Tiny bubbles of calm knowing,
When all I can feel is the frizzle
Of scorched fishes inside this black bowl of dust?

35 *Summer*

Wallflowers scorching blood in July
And the mother knitting
Tipped steel together
Clinks
Like whistling gnats
Out there on the sun lounge
The girl
Clamps back
The weight of her love for him
Which unexpressed
Now lies scorched into the field of grass
Where ghosts creep around in fear
That all will soon be over.

36 *Bubble*

At one o'clock,
Head swollen to a bubble,
People milling on either side were cardboard figures,
Burnt into the golden air,
Trapped by the smiles all around
In a time sandwich between morning and afternoon;
Nothing could touch them,
And the cars that swept along the road
Flick away the dust, that had settled on the black tarmac,
So that the ground was brushed clean of decay.

37 *Lunchtime*

Walking one by one
Down the white concrete blocks of kerbside,
I see such shiny rectangles on all sides,
Rushing past.
There is always the moving onwards,
Even the grey flecks on the ground jerk zigzag
Beneath my shrinking eyes
And pedestrians sweep past,
Curl around the shops like heaps of dandelions,
Carelessly bent with the weight of shopping baskets.
No silence in the coughing air
No stillness in the shuffle of wacky phrases,
The wind against the double glazing
At the end of the street a four-storey tower
Rises high, a whitewashed crack against the water sky
And sways.
No-one is ever motionless
No city ever rests at any time,
Not even a flat patch of parkland.
Each stone vibrates,
Seeks to reach out,
Just as I do now,
Through the opaque brain
To someone in the city, someone I love.

Cellophane sandwiches, cold sausages and brown apples,
Boots shuffle to the counter,
Camel-hair elbow prods to the front,
Crinkle of hairs pink
Against the spoons.
Outside lorries grumble
From Holborn to Surbiton and back again.
A dog weaves through the queue,
Whirs its head
And totters out into the blind light.
Fingers prod a totem of stitches onto plastic handles.

38 *Crowd*

Brown and pink arms
And faces,
Rushing to catch buses,
Teeth aglow in haste,
But not smiling;
Perambulators in Brixton
Roll over squares of paper.
A yellow plastic bag
Upon a pushchair
Crossing the road
On wheels of silver.
I remember now all the evil,
That is in me,
It rises up like a pebble,
Black and shiny.
A shopkeeper's angry voice re-echoes
Beneath the yawn of buses.
The crowd
Moves forward
Like a centipede,
Unrepentant.

Hate to be in a crowd
Hands pressing on all sides,
Indented fingers in my back,
An elbow upon my buttock.
Degradation abnormal,
Yet is this so?
Perhaps the truth of concentration-camp normality,
Bodies no longer individual,
Artificial self-respect for the box of air we walk in.
Now
Shame and distaste annihilated
Along with six million Jews,
I forget my body
And subsist.

39 *The Blind Man*

Rush-hour malaise.
Slow plodding of feet on all sides
Through the tunnel. Hypnotised
By the rhythmical tread, thighs jerking up and down,
Puppets we advance, a day of boredom stretching ahead,
Our senses silenced.
In the middle of the crowd a blind man
Chats eagerly to his escort.
'Tim took his bicycle to the garage this morning.'
Attempts to be normal, one sense lacking,
Vivacious.
Perhaps his belief in God necessitated and justified.
We respond to him as a friend,
No longer barricaded against each other,
Victims of the rat-race.
A stab of love kindled by his white stick
And by his ignorance that with faculties intact
Harmony comes seldom.

40   *Off Peak*

In the peak of the rush-hour
The man sat down next to me,
Squat, fat and jostling.
Broke a tacit rule
And chewed his fingers.
Then with a file,
He scraped the nail.
White slithers.
Dull fatigue, off peak I watched
In hatred.
Then a decision. The choice of free will,
I decided to like him,
To switch the will into a different gear,
Like the antennae aerial of a television set.
To push the steel rods down to the left
With a quick motion.
I began to like him
And as the crumbling nail-dust
Rolled off onto his trousers,
Flake upon white flake,
So my hatred diminished
Into a clean-cut half-moon of civility.

41 *The Joke*

A man and a woman in a restaurant,
Waiting for coffee.
He joked.
She sighed. It was more of a wail than a laugh,
A scream of pain
To see the link between the two ideas,
The normal coin and its counterside, the absurd
Crudely interwoven.
Her laughter was loud
To crush all future attempts
At such cool impudence,
Breaking the horizontal line of her day
From morning to noon to evening to night,
Each portion linked with squares, different yet fitting,
Pastel greens and blues of a patchwork quilt,
To keep the sleeper warm.
Not a moth-eaten old fur coat
Thrown over the blankets by mistake.
No taste, so primitive, so underbred.
He will not make the same mistake again.

42   *The Bore*

I thought of you, picking grapes,
The white glow of skin hot upon lucid green,
And as I picked I sucked one grape from every bunch
To test for sweetness.
Gradually I reached the end of the fence of vines,
And the sugar began to grow sour against my tongue,
Cloying acid.

43 *Kibbutz*

Lime teeth,
Straw of grass,
Stunned beneath the fanwater,
As the hose pours down.
Could I shed this chalk skin,
Peel off into brown health,
Like the women in sun-chairs on the lawn,
Chattering,
Arms and elbows fat,
Move around evading babies?
Sun, hot-glazed behind the Wedgwood sky
Crackles the avocado tree
And weeds that prickle
Beneath long toes.
Men move slowly from place to place
Dangling long bodies, tiny hips
And swinging from lazy shoulders.
Hot dust melts,
Cotton shifts, dry soft,
Cling folds;
Reach out
Loops of guttural laughter,
Quacks the argument in half.
Criss-cross of lime and earth-clods,
Scorched huts on the patchwork,
As the kibbutz
Burns new friends
Onto its open face.

44 *Vacuum*

In a café by a window
There is no thought.
Transparent mind mirrors the world outside,
Jumps off the edge of the world,
Topples over from the corner of the square earth
Before Galileo demolished it.
Down into the black smoke
I dissolve into the tight threads
Of the blue linen tablecloth
And smudge the filigree plant pot window
With my collapsing atoms,
That permit this anachronism.

45 *Trafalgar*

Pause,
While London changes,
Here in the central square
The fountains
Lift a gleaming dish of Trafalgar water
To placate some Anglo Saxon god
Baffled
At this usurping traffic;
Streams of hoodlums perched astride
The pepper and salt stone
Defy the thrust
Of spiked water-gates,
That will never let through the sixteenth century,
While nearby
In walled galleries,
Huge colour snapshots
Linger on forever
In heavy frames.

46 *Outsize*

The fat shopper in the fitting-room
Stares at her contorted self in the glass.
Her wishful eyes, like lenses, narrow the bulges
To plumpness,
And then as the retina readjusts,
Invincible accuracy of the optic nerve,
She sees again the curves of rubbery pink,
That dent at the touch
And then fill out again,
Like sandcastles sinking in the sea.
They assert their validity
Despite the prospect of hunger-cramping weeks to follow
And her angry sigh as she squeezes out
Of the much too little black dress,
Reminds her that in a different century
This swollen goodness
Might have been recognised as such.

47 *The Enemy*

The challenge of an enemy,
To recognise the black shadow that approaches
And step calmly onto its surface.
Do not be deceived,
When the dark outline fades into the twilight,
A treacherous invisibility,
Convinces you that animosity is not your problem,
Your warm, frank smile and a life of channelled effort.
But the shadow will return beneath the hot sun
Of beating midday,
Black against the white sand.

PART III

AFTERNOON

48 *A Flock of Blackbirds*

        A flock of blackbirds
        They cry and cry
        And turn and turn about the sky
        They fall down on the brown fields
        Where the farmer's plough
        Has turned the worms
        And up they fly
        Blackbirds
        In a crowd
        I hear them call
        I see them all.

The wind is blowing on my window
And a voice seems to come from nowhere.

49 *Dragons' Teeth*

After the broad road,
White as a pillar of salt,
Where the taxi throws a black hearse portent
Into the dust of the lunch-hour hush,
Back to the office;
The typewriters lined like dragons' teeth,
Wary and waiting.
The clerks blackened by fatigue,
Patter and flick of the wrists,
Knit a pattern,
Plain as looped handwriting
And pearl as the spots of sunlight
On the polished legs
And cornered tabletops.

50 *Street Dance*

The crazy sect are dancing
Along the corner of Oxford Street.
It is four o'clock on a Wednesday afternoon.
Why do they dance and sign and jingle bells,
Trailing their pink robes along the dust-tracks
Left by the swish of wooden sandals?
Why do they flick their wrists
And nod their bald heads
Into a row of shaven sandy pumpkins,
When everyone in the offices above
Is cramped within the magnetic sphere
Of individual braincells
Ticking the minutes away?
Here in the streets a few passers-by chat hurriedly
And up there in the executive suite
The secretaries swap streaks of conversation,
Lassoing one personality onto another,
But here on the corner the whole group of dancers
Have lost their selfhood
In the clacking feet of communal jollification.
Bells jingle up and down
And there is nothing left to do but laugh
At the splash of pink robes that sway to and fro endlessly
Like goblins clamped to a gigantic metronome.

51 *Stifled*

Tepid afternoon tea-leaf air
Fills the nostrils.
Two girls, drowsing over their typewriters,
Fling the windows open wider
To let in a finger of same-temperature breeze,
Cannot be felt or smelt.
Unrefreshed, they breathe deeper,
Reassured by the placebo
And wonder whether this is the C-major scale of living,
Which they too often evade
And find again with the stale nod of familiarity.

52 *Friday Afternoons*

Untidy Friday afternoons,
Ends of withered roots sprouting anew
Seeds
For the following week,
Unconcluded. Slow fatigue
Aching neck, backbone extended.
To flop into Saturday
The wish
Dwindles
Beneath letters to type, forms to amend.
A joke. Slow to understand
The laugh.
Convulsions of giggles like the spiral
Of an old jack-in-the-box.
A lorry passes.
Spiky details of bureaucracy
No longer matter.

53 *Interruption*

Bank holiday Monday, white afternoon, no milk.
The Indian grocers on the corner always open.
Teenage boys of graded height serving
And filling up the trays lethargically.
I stand by the till and hand over a five-pound note.
Three silver coins for change.
My outstretched palm touches the till,
Mesmerising him to open it again.
Slowly the crisp green and white paper
Crackles in his hand,
And the jagged teeth grin unevenly
Beneath black dot eyes
And oily black hair.
He wakens into laughter at this challenge
And kicks the spicy bags of yellow grain at his feet.
Green leaf aromas blend into the tepid air
And a man runs past the window pulling a barking dog.

54   *Bank Holiday*

The park on Easter Monday
Is dripping green
From oily trees,
That clamour into a rustle of drops
Over the path of stones;
Scrape of heels against
A dragging perambulator
And crunched decisions
To spend more time in the open air,
Away from the boxes of brick,
That leak stifled air
And never grow warm,
While here the silvered flesh
Gleams like peach fish
Against flapping raincoats
And little boys screeching to kill.
Now
The third eye opens
To hear a trail of bouncing footsteps,
Which will never
Ever
Reach their destination.
There is a splintering of wood
Into benches of planks,
That hold secure,
And whistling birds
Too wind-shaken
To be afraid of satiation.

55 *Park-Time*

Sunday afternoon.
Out of the glass-porched house,
Down the high street.
Empty,
Whispering solitude,
Into the warm-air park.
Stockinged feet cool against the grass,
Twigs and black lumps of damp soil.
A brass band plays cheerful marches,
Each portion framed by rows of deckchair clapping.
Toes wriggle against a prickly twig.
A girl shouts with laughter,
As a ball is thrown between her legs.
Sustained trumpet roar of military climax,
As the old week dies and with sharp birth pangs,
A new week emerges.

56 *Rainy Day in the Tourist Season*

Through bleary latticework of rain
The trees in stilts yawn up to stretch
A Wedgwood willow pattern against the glass plate
Of the city square.
Inside the gallery
St Peter lifts up a heavy key,
And the air is filled with Kentucky surprise
And gold frescoes;
At the other end of the town
The traffic is waterlogged into a tight jam,
A circle of grey blocks beneath the drizzle,
Trapped like a swarm of rats.

57 Misunderstanding

The coach is flashing through the hills
In the grinding heat.
'Open the door. I'm stifling,'
Shouts an indignant voice from the left.
'Leave it shut. I don't like the draught,'
The old woman splutters.
An arm swings the door open and emerald green
Floods into the mouldering pool of sunlight by my feet.
'It's draughty,' growls the old woman.
I stare at her absently, thinking of
The overlapping speckles of green and yellow.
A Van Gogh two o'clock
Is blazing through the open door.
She intercepts my stare
And her eyes, strange violets,
Throw a pool of suave indignation
Onto my lap,
Sparkling.
'It's not my fault I'm old and feel the draught.'

58 *Shadows*

I have known you in another life.
I delve down to the roots of some pleasant land
Before this womb's existence.
Green fields and shapeless pink huts,
Sunlight and the smell of wallflowers.
Silence of the afternoon.
The fresh winds blow
Into the empty spaces.
I see you shambling aimlessly across the grass
And then through a sheet of shadows
A cold winter,
And your slow movements as you shuffle up and down
Like a caged dog.

59 *Pity*

Pity
Passes through the layered consciousness,
Like butter drenched from cows
In the sunlight;
Speeded up film
Grasps
In one grope through the strings of orange rooftops
Concrete slabs of offices,
Through the ocean of glass water,
Where fish and corpses rot,
Breaks through the night,
The ticking brain,
The thinking eye,
Snaps
Everywhere
In a camera-shot.

60 *Bones*

His anger murdered her with eagle eyes,
Clipped her into white silence.
For three days she was empty,
Dried out to ivory like a bone gleaming dry
On the sands,
Curiously
Clean,
Until the sea released from its freeze,
Jerked back again into rhythm,
And there were new faces beneath the sun.

61 *Meeting*

Changed.
The white skin was still the same,
But the features were compressed, severe,
Throwing away the past in a pinch of breath.
The flame of her rain-blue eyes had flattened into a fish
And ten long years of adulthood
Had left her limpid white.
No rain was falling that October day,
When her shoes clicked into
The old familiar pattern by the kerbside,
A paper's edge away from danger,
Still the same
As the cars groaned by,
While rain moisture hung in the air,
Clung to the steel-white sky,
Impending pain,
And her washed-out skin,
Hollow of thinking cheek and curve of bone,
Grew old,
As I stared, wondering what had caused this alteration.

62 *Fishing*

His poised
Eyes,
Leaping fish.
Fringes of
Curtained eyelashes;
Behind
A small boy waits
To return to the green triangles of fish and weed,
Pull up clods of earth and spiky grass,
Damp smell of mould,
From where the worms curve out
Under the slimy boulders.
Blue iris curved into a marble of water
Looks out
Perplexed,
Middle-aged.

63 *Time Machine*

Red telephone kiosk
Leaning against the waving elm at the corner of the street,
Which of you will fall down first?
Perhaps vandals will remove your panes of glass
From between the red bars,
Or perhaps Century Twenty-One
Will demand a new kiosk colour,
Yellow or turquoise green.
Maybe a storm will crack your branches,
Fractured limbs straddled across the road,
Or a land-development scheme
Will demolish you both with a paper-plan.
If only I could come back and see this corner
In fifty years' time.
If I could only come back and see this corner
In five hundred years' time.

64 *Boredom*

Cold feet on an office afternoon.
Vacant sun shining onto my desk.
Void of thought after an early lunch
And five more hours ahead.
The afternoon asserts itself defiantly.
Choice of subject for thought.
Efficiency suggests a detailed analysis
Of the papers on my desk.
This norm perversely rejected,
The other extreme to be an invisible nun
And think a five-hour prayer.
But no. A lack of conviction.
I let my mind trickle in all directions
To break down the dikes that enclose it.
Perhaps a flood of images
Will swim up from the subconscious sphere,
Strange blackness.
The sun gleams on my hair,
A passive falling down into the pit,
Down, down, down, where no thought is possible,
Only to work mechanically and enjoy
The warm silk of the air flickering against my wrists
In the stillness of the afternoon.

65 *Teatime*

Blue-aproned lady waddles to and fro,
Shoes flapping, forearms
Plump from three decades of polishing,
Hums a song,
Waves in her right hand a rock-solid teacup,
White gleaming against the sodden teacloth,
At four o'clock, her muddled snatches
Of old-time pop songs
For the frisking hour.
Clink and tinkle of teaspoons.
Swish of tea,
Biscuit brown with well-being.

66 *On the Steps*

Sunflayed,
Cross-kneed upon steps.
That fall in piano-layers
Between two buildings,
And a street running between
With an iron gate
Wrought over
With gold upon black;
Smoke and burning kneed,
Threesomes drifting along the flagstones,
And the clap of shoes against stone,
As the cars fleece the roads,
Dustily whining.
White is the sun,
All wishing
Washed away
Against pillars,
Turning the dead Greek faces
Of the building
Into life.

67 *Museum Piece*

Charcoal drawings
Fading into fibres;
Through Venetian blinds
And wired squares of window
Strips of pink blossom
Catch onto birds' wings.
Outside, the May silence
Is punctuated by metallic whistling,
And indoors the buzz of
Hidden heating
Stifles
Into artificial torpor,
Italianate in London;
While clinging to walls
Muscled arms grip spears and nosegays
In bunches of brown ink.

68   *Silk-Worm*

A jade silkworm in the gallery,
Slippery green glass
From the Chou dynasty,
Takes me back to a pinpoint in the earth,
Centuries ago;
And the mirror of time is cracked
Into the tiny smithereens of jade pottery in this case,
That nail me down with glass pins back into the past.

69 *Growth*

Cats spawn kittens.
Sun ties cellophane of gold
All around.
I read a book, that grows,
Turns me to tree.
I am that book.
Question rises mammoth
To question.
This earth is too small a glove.

70 *Downpour*

Down sticks of rain,
Neck gasping fish,
Eyes bubble-bath.
Trapped in a museum-cased of glass
I see the fish and chip shop
Caught between two picture palaces,
Hacked away slice by slice,
Lie like the old silent movies
Dumbly in skulls,
Beaten back into the earth
By sticks of glass.

71 *Lost Between Stone Basins*

Lost between stone basins
And lions reaching out
To marble stairs.
The museum is so cool;
The perfect place to grow amazed
By turmoil
And concealed doors.
Where keys click into wooden cases
And strong men in black serge
Wind away for ever
Around turnings.
A fountainhead of fear
Pulls away from the crowd
Plaiting queues of enthusiasm
And tries to find the way out.

72 *Age*

This dismembered leg
From an ancient dynasty
Has seen better days.
Now weathered in pink stone,
It sits placidly upon its stand
And waits to be admired,
As it was
Many years before this audience,
An octogenarian,
Who, envious of its immortality,
Coughs a bronchitis sigh
And shuffles away,
Discomforted.

73 *Those Who Do Not Question Much*

Fools
That grin and have faith,
Why did not their matted brains
Grow to such convolutions
As those who scheme
And force their own design
Upon the escaping day?
Those who do not question much
Are carried along by the traffic
That forks through ribbons of trees,
Where the buildings crumble to grey
And tell of the hours
Trapped in the sunlight,
As they wait for the changing patterns of dust
Upon the stone.

74 *Ephraim*

Ephraim in his bedsitter
Smooths out onto grained skin
And moves slowly from chair to chair.
Behind lime curtains
The afternoon
Listens.
The television-set throws two comediennes
Bearing double chins
Onto a heap of textbooks
Below.
A poster of a girl in rags
Above a cricket calendar
Marks the days away
Without surmise.
Only the weekly cheque
To spin along
A new friendship
And clothes of lines and silk
That hang in fine squares
Against the positioned shadows
Of these four walls.

75 *Malaise*

Walking away from the doctor's maisonette,
Through the reconstructed road and the scaffolding,
The surgery to the buildings falling to pieces
Stone by stone,
I remembered the man in the waiting-room,
Baggy trousers flopping against the chair's
Caramel wooden legs,
And the doctor's tired monotone next door.
Through the side-streets the silence
Pounded against my ears,
Despite the crouching boys by the lamp-post,
Playing games with pieces of old branch,
Scratchily against the ground,
Leaving cuts in the soft soil-dust,
Tiny clouds of earth against the wrought-iron gate nearby
And it seemed for a second that all the world
Was mouldering away.

76 *Verdure*

Hatred dwells among people,
Like cheese growing mould,
Turns green,
Corrodes
To old bronze;
Forgotten candlesticks
Unearthed from a Roman site
Can never more spit yellow spears of flame,
But quiescent
Swallow within their stems
The hostile dead,
That hissed
Before their enmity was swollen
To surprised love,
Trapped hypnotic
In the green afternoon light.

77 *Parasite*

In France
The mistletoe sprouts on oak trees
Like birds' nests
Thrown into the branches by mistake
Against the metallic sky;
Lives parasitical and swells guilty.
Falling leaves in autumn
And winter nakedness a reminder
That it must share the bleakness
Of sparse times.

78 Double Biology

Thursday afternoons are for double biology,
Green afternoons, like old hot water bottles.
The weather is cloudy April but hot, without ventilation,
And the experiments are slow, plants to be dissected;
A messenger is sent to fetch new specimens
And we wait in silence while the teacher
Moves wrist over wrist the objects around her desk.
The girls in the front row are all in pink stripes,
Pyjama material,
To sleep away this hot water bottle afternoon.
The salamander larvae are swimming round
The brown water of the tank
Between slimy ferns and black twigs,
Shrubs of the waterworld, where all is curling
Away into wriggling life.
Through the window the oak trees swell into
A heap of emerald triangles
And a man pulls his dog sharply around the corner.
We are bottled into this room
And our thoughts wriggle through the air
Like the tiny worms that dazzle the retina
From the afterglow of a white window.
Thursday afternoons are safe and slow
As the teacher moves the objects
Wrist over wrist around her desk
And the salamander larvae dissect the brown water
And move slowly around the black twigs
And under the slimy ferns.

79 *Old Woman*

Scrawny blue-veined hand still clutching
Patent leather navy handbag,
Salmon mac of plastic squeaking
Rhythmically in time to speaking,
Every inch communicating,
Voice and gesture loudly stating
Friendly, yearworn female outlook.

Rumbling down the rainy roadway,
Bus encloses crowded gaggle
Of commonsensical old women,
Compromised to life, but gaily,
Though the body ages sadly,
Triviata compensating
Often loving, rarely hating,
Ugliness accepted gladly.

Acrimonious and bitter she was to me last year,
Her tired feet aching, the weight of years, jealousy,
Now on a summer's afternoon,
Mellowed, her face is an older reflection of mine,
Thin lips, flickering surprise.
Impossible to hate one's mirror,
Every face will echo upon the next,
A microcosm, universal glass,
Woes upon word upon action.
So in silence she walks past,
Forgiving and empty.

80 *Lemon*

On a primrose day in March,
When frost was mindlessly forming on the shrubs
Like bread-mould at the end of a long, stale day,
A whiff of raindrops fell from the sky
And crystallised mid-air into an icy lemon.
Four feet from the ground it hung
In steady levitation
A spray of dust drifting from nearby
Covered it with particles of grit and labelled it
Inedible, unfit for human consumption.
Dusty lemon, I will partake of you,
Though soiled and grimy,
For I need your pungent grip
To teach me a secret.

As soon as I sip the juice
I discover the source of life's vitality.
It lies in a careful balance between waking and sleep
Taut energy and slack leisure,
The thinking will, the contemplating mind,
All is juxtaposed in the invisible hypotenuse of a triangle,
The active and the passive in harmonious antithesis.

The rain is falling silently on a primrose day in March
It washes away the dust and the grime,
Leaving the lemon pure and unobtrusively symmetrical.

81 *To Forestall*

The railway line of life.
Never to be off-guard.
A sunny four o'clock.
Light streams into the green fields,
Yellow fingers of light.
The sheep and the cows asleep.
Vacuum of peace illusive.
Beyond, a rubble of old contorted metal
Wreckage of a car
Thrown onto the line that morning.
A prank or perhaps a crime?
This is the problem of disaster.

82 *Acorn*

When all the love has dwindled away
And sucked you dry as an acorn shell,
Rolling downhill in the dust on a September afternoon,
Clods of earth tumbling in the flickering wind,
The cut of splintering twigs against the ground,
Only then can you feel the empty wind,
Battering blue bulbs of air, unearthly vacuum,
And know that the only thing that endures
Is the kernel point, grit in the nucleus,
Spirit of love that sucks up the dust into a blanket,
A wave of river return.

83   *Saturday Afternoon*

Cricklewood in dust, garbage gleaming in the sun,
Frying like sizzled New York afternoons,
Click over the pavestones
In search of a handbag shop,
Painted blue, that no-one remembers;
Pulled along different streets
By false advice, and caught in a web of sun-steam
And crackling shopping-bags.
The boy in the paper shop
Wrinkles his nose with fluff
And the girl, red-faced over National Health spectacles,
Beams a frank perspiring smile
And shakes her hair over the road,
Two West Indians with raised shoulders
Discuss the sharp guy they met last week,
Cars glint sneering windows
That slip across London out of the zigzag
Documented file of pedestrians,
Whose budgetary achievement is an ideal
To be discarded, when at six o'clock
They leave the streets scattered
Into twosomes and threesomes.
As the traffic falls to rest,
And the coinomatics
Hospitable to the last,
Draw in new clients
Swinging
Polythene corpses.

84 *Bus*

The bus is swamped with raincoats, shopping bags,
Overlapping folded linen gloves and packages of cartons.
The bus conductor, out of temper,
Screams to bulging crowds,
Who usurp illegal stances on the top deck
And around the stairs,
Until after three minutes order prevails again,
Men and women sit in neat rows,
Subdued by their momentary chaos,
Relieved by their confusion
Like children rushing out of school into the neat vicinity
Of drawing-rooms.
Past the windows
Flash shops and neon lights,
Pretty secretaries and scruffy pedestrians.
Silence along the rows of upholstered benches,
The peace of observation as the six o'clock world
Swings past along with the traffic
And the newspaper-sellers,
The quiet anticipation of the evening,
Possibilities of dinner parties, theatre-outings or
Quiet hours spent in front of a black and white box,
Which is as lively as the reality
Along the side-streets and byways.

Suddenly a tramp clambers to the front seat,
Stands bolt upright and declaims religious propaganda,
Hellfire and darkness await for those
Who do not repent.
Titters of mirth among the sleepy rows upon the benches
No condemnation for a drunkard
But pity for his manner,
And yet there is a slow change among their ranks
Of purchases and pleasures,
A faint fear of his sheltered mind
That has been a possibility.

85 *Hunger*

An all-devouring void inside me bleats
And moans for food to fill the empty gap.
Hunger swells a million far-off souls,
We care not, until pain begins to tap
At our own plump selves and then a true
Insight arrives of what they must go through.

When I reach home I'll eat a juicy steak,
Bowls full of creamy soup and fruit to follow.
At present I'm alone in the cruel, grey rain.
Outside I'm chilled and inside a mere hollow.
I never thought I'd feel such misery,
A dreary ache, a demi-agony.

And when I've eaten I will send a cheque
To some worthwhile deserving charity,
And then I'll feel a kind, expansive glow
At helping those who thirst continually.
Meanwhile all my most altruistic wishes
Are drowned in a host of contemplated dishes.

86 *Food-Time*

Taken by surprise
I squirm,
As the man opposite me in the restaurant
Begins to lash out at eating, feet flying in all directions,
Head bent into the plate and elbows protruding;
A splutter and a squeak and a bang on the plate
And he is transformed into a large pink pig,
Flapping ears and curly tail in the air.
The waitress looks at him in surprise,
As his tiny eyes blink
With the dripping of peas onto the floor
And the smoky formica table squelches with mud,
As his palms stretch out exhausted for the next course.

87 *The Waiter*

This restaurant is like a fore-echo
Of an automated world to come.
The waiter serves up each course with clinical precision,
Hovers cautiously watching the last crumb of fish
To be swallowed
And leaps forward to exchange
The old plate for a new one.
I feel like a battery hen
Or a four-year-old,
Whose physical progress
Is a source of constant observation.
In obedience I munch in rhythm with the servings
And leave the restaurant with some of my individuality
Assassinated.

88 *The Waitress*

You work long, steaming days here
Serving up plates of food
To an ever-changing public that consumes it
Minutes after its preparation.
Who is to prove that you have actually worked here,
When the food and clientele are never twice the same?
Admittedly one pink face may resemble another
And one plate of Yorkshire pudding
Is scarcely different from its neighbour,
And one white-aproned waitress gone like the next.
I know you are the same,
Because I have stamped your card
With weekly efficiency for the past six similar years,
But does anyone else?

89 *Cactus*

Potted plant between the lace of curtains
And fingerlets of frost upon the pane
The years go by for people in restaurants,
Streams of green vegetables turn into days
Of bedsitter waiting;
A cactus life,
As the leaves curl in one upon the other
In overlapping succulence.
Cars outside the window gleam blue and shining
Speeding towards the city centre.
Here on the outskirts
It is peaceful, insulated
And the waiter is always the same,
Once a shy boy, now placid with rotundity
From years of waiting upon pale loiterers,
Who sit and watch the potted plant
Between the lace curtains
And fingerlets of frost upon the pane.

90 View

Frost and fog through the windows
Turn the trees to an older decade
Caught leaning at an angle,
Weighed down with leaves and spikes,
Berries jostling in the grass around the trunk
And an old blue door, painted through dusty air
Eternally upon the memory of anyone
Who may care to pass.
Not an atom lost
In the archival chambers of the brain.

91 *Pier*

Walking, windswept
Over the slatted pier
I see the blue beneath the gaps
And above a frozen sky
Of united cloud;
Couples huddled on deckchairs,
Icy smiles on rigid cheeks
My companion takes out a book
And reads on the wooden bench,
Ignoring sea, sky, spray
And I feel
A gust of solitude.

92 *Six o'clock*

Curiously
Relieved I stare at the knife and fork touching at the tip,
Arms pointing together in a demure lap.
Egg and tomato ketchup play Van Gogh
On the plate, and a small frill of grey egg-white
Turns it into a Salvador Dali.
A pop song plays the working day out,
And the drum beat release from the spell
Of routine.

93   *Flight*

The birds wing jerkily across the mauve dust of the sky,
Where the houses touch the spidery trees.
They gallop away over the curve of the air
And lose all dignity,
Bouncing,
The chords of life broken,
No need to make the primeval journey to the south.
Today they have burst free to swerve wildly
In a star,
High above the railway track,
Watching the incoming trains
Move sleek as a snake down the line.

94 The Stones

At certain times of the day,
The time of the stones,
We are alone,
When the waves roll away for westwards down the shore
And the pebbles are naked in the slanting sun rays,
All heaped together in an endless marble upon flint
And always the stones are alone.
It comes when he sees it holds no menace,
Gentle roll of water,
Glint of red veins upon the rocks,
Sweep into the runnels of pounding waves
To discover anew the strange wet sky
Falling into the charcoal water
And the hiss of sizzling chinks of glass
From a broken bottle.
Sweating to bloodboil in the shaft of heat
That brushes down the shingle,
Clink and crunch as the stones fall from the cliffsides
To nestle into a horizontal hold
Clink and crunch as they settle into endless patterns.

PART IV

EVENING

95 *Label*

Walking over the grass on an evening in June,
After the cider in the pub,
With him on one side and her on the other,
Our heads bubbling like marbles,
Opaque though shimmering behind turquoise glass,
I let the seven o'clock sunlight
Simmer into a yellow dazzle and held his hand.
The girl on the other side whispered,
'My God, he's a Hampstead Liberal.
I can't stand them, they get on my nerves.'
She laughed from the corner of her large lips,
And the yellow and green waves of light
Began to settle into spots and shapes,
As my thoughts coagulated into leaves
And blades of grass.
Everything seemed sharpened and minimised,
He was no longer a warm shape at my side,
But a sociological concept
Like the Indians, the Jews, the Anarchists, the refugees,
And as the shapes around me
Solidified into painful clarity, he dissolved.
I turned round to the girl at my side
And smiled back at her
Lopsidedly, in unwanted imitation,
And wondered what would happen
If the wind changed
And my face remained contorted thus forever,
What would she label me?

96 *Summer Evening*

Beyond the footlights of the open-air theatre
Tucked into an alcove of trees,
The puns on stage grow quicker, more raucous
Every moment,
And the wild gulls above
Moan and wail in the wind,
Blocking out the laughing students, the grey scenarios,
And the purple and green satins
Converting *Twelfth Night* into a tragedy of errors.

97   *Tube*

The Tube on a Saturday evening.
No thoughts, only red and yellow jumpers
And a purple coat,
That makes me blink.
The girls opposite giggle
And we are all held down in our seats
By a cloud of warm, smoky air.
No annoyance,
Only a breathing in and out in unison
As the floating colours make nonsense
Of the discarded, thinking week.

98 *Image*

Walking between the great stone buildings of Holborn,
I see in focus
The heavy flagstones
And street-signs in black and white,
The plastic shoes rotating along trays
Through double glazing
And the rain falling softly
On this Saturday evening,
Sweeping clean the revolving doors
And thirsty gutters,
As people in the distance walk in pairs
Heading for drawing-rooms
And pubs and clubs along the way.
I cannot see beyond to the century before this façade,
Or afterwards,
When it will take another posture;
But know only the splash of water
Against rubber heels;
While in another room
The man I love
Sees beyond all this
And shares it with another.

99 *The Evening Class*

The silence has been broken
By a string of sentences, that shuffle out in monotony
Lisping like snakes, that hiss in single
The words rise and flow,
Fall softly around the circle of faces.
The lightbulb pares away the flesh,
Leaving the bones exposed
Beneath its lemon shine;
Grows brighter, as the voices rise in argument;
Brown growl of indignation
Crackles like roast beef.
Performs a startled chirp,
Coughing splutters out like water in an agitated pipeline
And a thin trickle of laughter grows
Until the torrent of conviction
Beneath the hanging ceiling
Quickens and exhausts itself into silence.
A cough;
Space of time to reflect the quiet possibility,
That every idea can be considered in many ways.
The light flickers.

100 *Routine*

No better than the next
We rise and fall;
When evening casts a celluloid
Sheet of brown dust.
Goldfish perceptions flick their fins
Inside the goldfish bowl of mind.
The daily grind
Is a Nazi task
To shift a heap of pebbles up a mound
And pull them down again.
Scapegoating whosoever blocks the path
With idiosyncrasies.
The fish swim around a dizzy circuit
Orange and gold and flecks of green,
Glimpses,
That break through the double glazing of thought
Into the subconscious.
Down there
A black kaleidoscope shapes remembered faces
Into relief.
They mock the day
The glass is sundered,
Waves roll over the crushed splinters
Beneath the roar of traffic
Pouring home
Into the dark night.

101 *No Danger*

Her head is cider-swollen to a bubble,
As she staggers down the road after the concert,
Sleepy in the July torpor,
Ecstatic with the clang of the cymbals of the cantata.
Each step jogs like a burst of trombones
And the lamp-post throws a beam of yellow light
Onto her dilated pupils.
Across the road a familiar voice shouts,
'Come over here. I've got some news.'
Mesmerising her like the bulbs of light,
The clashing chords and amber liquid in the heavy mugs.
A streak of energy shoots through
Like the sizzle of an old battery.
She veers into the road and runs across,
Runs over the bulges of grey ground,
The tiny stones, the warm air.
A flicker of light catches her left eye
And she stops abruptly.
As a car swims down the road towards her.
She stops, hypnotised by the yellow headlights,
That gaze at her with the canny stare of an old frog.
Feeling no danger, drowsy, comfortable,
She looks lovingly at the bulky machine,
As it swims nearer and nearer, faster and faster,
Requesting her to move one way or the other,
But she resists and with a drunken hiccup wills it to swerve.
It veers to the right, submissive but only by law,
And she staggers to the pavement, giggling.

102 *Rosanna*

Rosanna is silent and blonde and haughty,
Her hair swept back into elegant neatness.
Her eyes are round and vacant and black.
Yet she has a meaningless kind of completeness.
Are you jealous? Well, she will not care
For she lives in a silent and cold eerie sphere.

Rosanna is working, mindlessly, quietly,
Working hard in the daytime to celebrate nightly.
Stars twinkle and flash in her empty, black eyes
As she wanders around in a fool's paradise
Are you jealous? Well, she will not care,
For she lives in a silent and cold, eerie sphere.

103 *Foretaste*

Something
Of Hell
I saw
With this woman
Here on the chair
Not in her.
But she knew of it;
Bird tattered whistling,
A fugitive pain,
Alone
In the brown light
That hung over endless
Rounds of space.
Whirring huge,
A scratch of a leaf,
Moaning
From somewhere alone,
Never to know
The next move,
What agony will bring.
Lost for ever and why everywhere
Must drown,
She cannot know,
But only feel;
Her mouth turned down
Not to cry,
And the ache of the huge pallid figure
In the evening room.

104 *Trendy People*

I thought she was[*] so cool, so untouchable,
Aristocratic chin jutting sideways
Against her green lace dress.
'I don't like them at all,' she said.
'I can't bear trendy people.'
Her eyes, brown almonds,
Glowed nutlike against her pale skin.
In my mind I shouted an angry thought at her:
Stop labelling things! Stop labelling people!
I noted the swollen contours of her cheeks
And catapulted the thought across the air
From my eyes to hers.
I screamed it, I bellowed it in silence.
Slowly she turned away and blushed,
Pink fingers of blood flowing into her throat.
'How silly I am,' she said.
'I don't suppose they're trendy at all.
And if they are, I don't suppose they can help it.'

---

[*] In an alternative 'second-person' version of this poem, this is written as: 'I thought you were so cool'.

105 *Hypnosis*

We lay in a circle on the carpet, heads pointing inwards,
A black box tape-recorder held us together,
A man's voice, slow and buzzing, chocolate black
Led us into a cave, where there were no walls
And no exit.
Further along in a horizontal
We were dragged into the gloom until
External thoughts were snipped away,
There was only the centre-point
Of being there.

106 *Bio-energetics*

Zany clown,
Red velvet jeans stretching over bony legs,
Leaping on the carpet up and down.
A trick gymnastic to roll away the tension
From the jerky muscles,
To roll away your manhood
And turn you into a goblin figure from a pantomime.
Infectious decadence.
The leaping figures around scream and shout.
The carpet ruffles and purrs
Beneath the long contorted toes,

107 *Last Respects*

Hidden in a telephone kiosk
On an evening in June, green leaves,
One chaffinch singing,
She stared at the red paint
To summon up some grief,
To pray after the death of an aunt. It happened
Two days ago.
Black telephone, a message to the dead,
Red paint and smeared squares of glass,
A pile of directories buzzing with print,
The evening buzzing with eight o'clock exhaustion.
A couple saunter by
Shoulder to shoulder.
There is no sadness, only fatigue.
Inside the flat
The family crowded, chair next to chair,
Laughs and gestures, elbow upon knee,
Shoes crossed, a circle of light gleaming upon
The black leather toe.
Intimacy of blood ties.
No regret,
Only to be united in remembrance of eighty-two years.
'It was a ripe old age.'
The prayers, a long chanting upon chanting,
The surprise of a gradual participation.
A clicking of the wheel into position.

108 *Shyness*

A shy polythene bag
Keeps the washing dry on the way to the launderette
And holds them together in one bundle.
Protection against the sheeting wind,
That could tear apart
The yellow bedspread turquoise sheets
And purple trousers,
Splaying apart the corduroy legs
With the practised ruthlessness of a torture rack;
But locked in their transparent container
They remain neat squares and oblongs,
And bounce together softly,
As I enter the twenty-four-hour launderette.

109 *Interior*

In this Victorian parlour
Eggshell walls and gilt picture frames,
Dust specks on the points of spiky ornaments
And long waxen candles,
That sink cosily into the past;
Within these four walls,
Each objects nestles comfortably into position,
The grand piano gleams and preens itself
Against the bay-window
And the velvet curtains are drawn into overlapping folds
To keep this century out
And preserve the illusion of the past.

110 Stepping Outside

Flames and torture-rack of a Tudor epic film
The first cold autumn day hits me,
As I step out of the cinema into Trafalgar Square,
Shaking off my skin
Like a rabbit scuttling out of its hutch
Into a cool bed of lettuce-leaves.
I run down the subway into the tube-station
To talk to a friend
And bury myself in the patchwork conversation,
Trying to obliterate
The band of fear around my forehead.

111 *Surprise*

I do not know whether I have the understanding of sight
All my knowledge drifts through a sieve
Into not knowing;
But sometimes in the black mud evening,
The trees of the city
Hiss and spit, like the pines of an old forest
Meshwork of filigree, that crackles with understanding
And although the green has scorched into black
Charred away into cinders
Beneath the ash-dust lies the whisper
Surprise of growing
That I have known in another life.

PART V

NIGHT

112 *Night*

On the boat pub
Pretentious
Sea curls lashing
Flared light caught
Up
And thrown back
Over
The laughing girls;
Words too fast pour out
Dropped
From the black evening
Quickly
After lager and
Some frankness
Had resolved the civilised game
Now
By the deck
He stares
Pondiferously
At the black mirror
Smithereened
Eyes rounded
The old North star
And a few familiar landmarks
Awaken nostalgia
While she waits
For his mood to change
To workaday good humour.

113 *Loss*

When the dog ran away in the middle of the night,
And through the broken gate and down the hill,
I stood in the garden beneath the bulging black sky
And shouted his name across the blanket of grass.
I felt a circle of ears beyond the trees,
A stillness over the olive flower-beds
And I knew in that second
That I was one person,
Locked up inside a bag of pink skin,
Inside the stretch of my heart,
That all the love I had ever felt
Was rolling away down the hillside,
A crowd of shadow-figures from the past
Were toppling away for ever
And gradually the black sky grew purple with stars,
As the spinning legs of the animal twitched up the hill
And stumbled back into the garden,
Dissolving the frozen magnet of the night
Into a sway of wind.

114 *Winter*

Who loves the grey tent of darkness
At nine o'clock on a winter's night,
When the houses are shaded and silent
And people whisper as they walk the streets,
When the air is soft and sensitive?

I love the shiny reflecting pools
On the muddy pavements crisply ringing
And the puppy, who stumbles and hurries home
To the warmth of a cosy living-room,
An oasis of colour and flickering heat
In the oddly hanging black expanse
Of nine o'clock on a winter's night
When the houses are shaded and silent.

115 *Midnight at the Station*

Midnight at the station,
Shadows disappearing,
Brightly lit carriages,
Journey through cloud and steam,
Crash of grinding wheels,
Onwards,
Bone-shaking over the glassy tracks,
Slits of yellow windows
From passing trains,
Lights pinpointed
From flats across the span of vision,
Lurches to a halt,
Engine still vibrating.
Two youths pause from chatter
To listen to the silence,
Then onwards,
Jogging,
Laughter and clapping hands,
Railroads ahead

116 *Platform*

Through the railings,
Beyond the rail-track,
People pass and cars sail by
Like blancmanges,
Maddened by the slowness of Sunday
Raindrops peeling away from the surface
Of the lime-trees and rusted brick,
Leave them varnished
As the stones, that lie in beaded heaps
Around the lamp-posts.
A train approaches,
Splits the dampness,
Snake approaching,
Scatters the leaves and iron and rooftops
Into a thousand screaming jewels
That grow orange beneath the penetrating smoke.

117 *The Fainting*

When the pain comes,
Gold spots upon the darkening curve
Of a new world,
The people all around
Jingle up and down and smile,
Doe-faced, gentle-eyed.
Wearing soft fabric clothes
According to the latest fashion;
While wrapped in bands of steel,
Blood and flesh swirl
To win the fight,
Pulling down the knees to jellied nausea;
Lost upon a cloud of will-power,
Only ten seconds until the train will stop
Graciously before a wooden bench,
There to stay the pain
Awhile against the dew thickening into night,
Rustling with passengers around the kiosk
And up the steps;
Leaves and cloud console,
Until there is focus once more into relief;
Humdrum to lose that other curved earth
Of flesh and blood and bone,
Septic and aching,
Melted away.
Watching from afar
The lighted faces revolve,
Red-lipped, clownish.

118 *Party Time*

The party was a slit of light under the door
A glazed falsehood,
Piercing the circular eyes, peeling away the candlelight,
Sparks and shocks
To blot out the night
And join the guests together
In receding effervescence
Until all bubbles exploded
And it grew dark,
Time for the nightly ghosts to begin their uneasy prowl.

119 *Party Games*

Party games are fun.
Let's throw away all inhibitions.
You take off your tie and I'll take off my shoes
And we'll sit opposite each other
On the orange carpet, soft tuffs ruffled,
And tell each other a secret,
Something we have never told anyone else before, ever.
How strange to keep a secret bottled up all this time.
Effervescence released in surprise.
Perhaps you will despise me and I will condemn you.
No, we reassure each other of party loyalty,
Bound together by the yellow light
And the black fingers of shadows on the wall.
Your eyes are large and grey, fathomless contradictions.
You tell me that you are not normally candid
Not even to yourself,
But keep your thoughts hidden in greyness,
Grey as your eyes and your reticence.
I am always honest, so this little game
Is no novelty for me.
We laugh and link hands.
A shadow on the wall
Reminds us that this is eleven o'clock.
It is night. Yellow light flickers.

INSIDE THE STRETCH OF MY HEART

Now on a Friday morning
Traces of dust on our faces,
Searing white light illumines
And magnifies all blemishes,
We walk from opposite ends of the cold street,
Eyes cast down,
Locked in our different compartment of thought,
We do not see each other at first.
But as we pass, our eyelids flicker for a moment
In distasteful recognition.
The day is too white for subtleties,
Too cold for shadows released by the sun.
Only the naked outlines of the shop fronts
And two people in a deserted street,
Perplexed by the scorching white light of the day,
Which mocks them for thinking
That party games are fun.

120 *Dream of Oxford*

Is it a nightmare or a dream?
I see against a black sky a towering block of bedrooms,
Patched with yellow squares of light.
Through the window-panes students crouch
Over half-finished essays,
Long dressing-gowns, black shadow silhouettes.
The yellow squares pull me back, back into the past.
The rustle of essay notes;
Fingers piling together heaps of paper,
Cunning manipulation.
There is the silence of jumping minds at midnight,
A forest of tiny words scribbled and never read again,
A buzzing of love-affairs dissected and later forgotten.
The weight of their united adolescence reaches out
To touch the sky,
But instead squeezes my ventricles, churning black gloves
And the three o'clock dream fizzles out
Into yellow sparks,
Leaving only blackness.

121 *Christmas Eve*

After the cinema,
The painted eyes and candy-wrappers,
The pavement smacked up hard and jerky,
Line after line, a patchwork quilt upon the stone,
Each cross was a complete integrity
Of right angles, stretched out endlessly
As the wind blew cold in a parallel track
And wave upon wave of acceptance
Flowed down the street.
No enmity or duality was there,
But all was swept up into a hammock of this moment,
Which will always be somewhere,
To be prised out hour after hour
And retrieved in a blink of the eyelid,
Cast down towards the brown air of the evening.

Christmas Eve,
Yellow flames upon the stove,
Yellow flames of power,
Light rising from the black hub,
The black nest, where it all began.
Some cradle I see in the criss-cross of metal,
The heat is all there is,
The love that swears and burns but will not burn out;
Can destroy only sometimes,
But leads onwards into the mess, the pulling depths.
The chewing flames twist out of the black air
Into the aura of birth.

122 *Reality*

A hidden chink,
Vulnerable
When the tide is out. The sea has ebbed
Far, far away along the stretches of white sand,
Leaving a row of naked footmarks,
A rubber balloon and an old tin can,
A heap of ordure,
The sleeve of a muddy shirt buried beneath the sand.
My faults exposed,
I can only stare at the dazzling whiteness
And wait for the tide to roll back,
Grey feathers upon white lace, the foam.
Once more protected,
I can forget the shock of this moment
And sleep
Until the next time.

PART VI

INDOORS

123 *Yoga*

After the visitors departed,
Slowly from the sofas in the sitting-room,
I cleared a space on the carpet
And began to stretch.
As arms reached high above head,
Muscles and tendons elongated,
From skull to toe,
I became a vertical line
And the earth that was grounded in my feet
Wanted to reach out
Above the distempered ceiling
To the black moth-eaten blanket of sky
That hung above
With no pretence.

124 *Mouse*

The mouse, a tiny grey ball of fur,
Has fallen asleep over its poisonous meal,
Is awoken by a pinch of rubber-gloved fingers,
Which fling it into the nearest wastepaper bin,
Yet gently, without crushing the little beast,
Moved perhaps by the tiny momentary squeak,
Which turns it into a child's plaything,
And thus demands courtesy.

125 *Insect*

The daddy long legs
Cannot scuttle quickly enough out of the primrose bath,
But confused by the artistry of modern plumbing,
Slithers up and down the shiny slopes,
A Nazi exercise.
The flailing legs dance a black wire can-can,
Half an inch above the steaming water's top.
I dredge from somewhere something of compassion
And slip a cool flannel beneath the whirring body.
It leaps onto the floor to find the reassurance
Of black and white squares,
As they fall into their familiar pattern of symmetry.
The wheeling legs slow down to a frozen hunch,
As I break through the barriers of four limbs
To the bafflement of a tiny, pointed world.

126 *Television*

Oh black and white machine of information,
Highly distracting to my concentration.
The book I read seems cold and full of lies,
While you are slyly mobile before my eyes.
I know you as a being one degree
Below the robot in the eternal hierarchy.
A robot can respond, but has no heart,
But you ignore me manacled to your art.
If only you were fruitful all the time
And I am not demanding the sublime,
But would prefer your noise to educate me,
Instead you jingle loud and irritate me;
For all too often you syncopate and crash
With what I shall entitle popular trash,
With violence and sex and ghastly comedy,
But since it's in demand, what is the remedy?
Instead I try to read without success,
For you are there to mock at me *sans cesse,*

127 *Reminder*

Sunday television, an Italian wartime movie,
The ranting mother, savage cheekbones,
And the raped daughter, eyes
Deranged by shock, pupils upturned.
I would like to upturn the volume louder and louder,
Until the metallic tubes and plastic knobs
Have fizzled out into an orange whirls of sparks,
Blue hiss of smoke,
Annihilating the droning tanks,
The square-shouldered satin evening gowns,
And the old women, black bundles,
Nodding to themselves.
They live on in miniature in the colour supplements,
Framed with suitable captions,
But the twenty-three-inch face
That speaks to me on the screen,
Pupils gazing into mine,
Is an intrusion.

128   *Passive Involvement*

Try to absorb
The news on television
Of a flood, a murder, a railway crash.
In my armchair,
Legs splayed and fingers sagging into torpor,
Slippers on the carpet spring up from time to time
With the resilient push of the woollen tufts.
To bear vicarious pain at all times
Is difficult.
A continual participation
In the throbbing line of people
Linked together problematically
Like a reel of cotton knotted at intervals.
The points are small, almost invisible.
Only the finger probing with careful thought
These networks of thread.
Not easy. Deliberate patience.
Effort of passive involvement.

129 *The Deaf Ear*

The pounding Beethoven,
Beats crotchets upon the beige carpet of the bedsitter.
And the girl shrieks above the waves of his lament
Into the mouth of the telephone,
Hearing neither the voice at the other end, suburbs away,
Nor the pleas of the composer a century ago,
Yet equally demanding.

130 *The Search*

Perhaps this daily journal,
Pages of red ink, words dwindling to horizontal scribble,
Each day marking a new encounter,
Perhaps this self-indulgence should not be allowed
By my better judgment,
But the finished notebook,
Flopping from the weight of total honesty,
The cast-off skin of my growing self,
Gives food to nourish the inner core of my being.

131 *Why Write?*

I wrote away at ease until the poets
Acquainted me with their new sophistication.
Unnerved and shattered by their subtle breadth,
I recognised with awe their cool finesse.
Why write, I thought, when what I write is limited
To the delicacy of a narrow woman's attitude?
I am not well acquainted with their jargon,
Nor can I jingle wittily and dirtily,
With illusions to the sensational and the bizarre,
But then with resignation I soon determined
To follow up my own particular pattern,
Resolve my individual themes and questions,
Well limited perhaps but still defined:
An accurate survey of a single mind.

132 *The Poet*

The poet looks   out
Of his head
Sieves   and
Synchronises experience
Catches here   a silver ball
And there   an eyelash sliver
Of upside down images.
His friend helps quiet a lot
With new catchy phrases
And the strong sally
Of criticism.
The poet is
Sometimes
Very happy   to think
New   verses
But mostly impatient
Waiting
Waiting   for it
To happen
Next.

133 *To Write*

His writing is more real to him than life.
It forms the daily marrow.
External details merely husk and skin.
Cushioned by the knowledge of this mechanism in him,
Which converts all pain to words, he lives
A false pleasure and smiles.

She writes sporadically to define the stabs
That cannot be resolved,
By others, perhaps, but not by her.
She suffers. But his grimace is worse.

134 *Writing*

After a long gap between poem
And poem
Invention strikes the automatic pen
As a bonus, a skill, devised to produce fancy words
Like an icing set tricked out by deft fingers.
These phrases bear no relation to the surprised author,
Who reads through the legible output
With the embarrassed scrutiny
Of a close relative.

PART VII

THE TEN DAYS OF PENITENCE

135 *The Ten Days of Penitence*

Slowly the evil
Has seeped into my soul.
Rusted.
I cannot feel an assurance,
That all is burnt out in the boiling
Of time,
But feel the rot.
I am no longer myself,
But a black shape
Against the shades of a water-mauve sky
In the middle of a swarm of black shapes,
Waiting
For the reckoning.

136 *Memory*

A frightening thing is memory,
Sometimes it has such intensity.
A moment of insight sparks up alive
And illumines the present with brevity.
But soon the glow is fully erased
And the mind is an empty black slate again.
Often when defects are overcome
And promises made and hates discarded,
We find that the following intricate day
Involves such triviality
That the spark is nearly obliterated,
Devoured by the fangs of petty routine,
Return and glow, each moment of worth
With kaleidoscopic density
To nourish and fill the continual need
Of my inner thirsting immensity,
And form a flashing, active will
Wherever I may breathe or be.

137 *Egg*

I am an egg.
A black band in the middle separates
The lower brown cup from the upper white.
Down below, the turbulence of the idd
Rages against the white shell of the superego
And they meet together in the black band,
The judo belt of the creative impulse.

138 *Roaming*

Pain produces logic
To anaesthetise
By justification;
What if this jumbled scream
Were nothing more
Than that,
A screaming jungle,
To roam among triangular leaves long hours
And never to find the hypotenuse?

139 *Filter*

Without the selectivity
Of a brain filter,
All experience flames upon the ground
Meaningless, chaotic,
An LSD trip misfired.
And so, with little finger elevated
I make a fastidious choice
And remain coherent.

140 *Brain*

Sharpen the brain
To a fine point of precision,
So that it sizzles with electricity
And in the coils of red glow
Insights will emerge
From the dazzle of unleashed thoughts.

141 *Jealousy*

The green eyes of the black tomcat stare into mine,
As I pour a carton of cream into a lopsided pan,
Flickering deprivation of white I possess
By right of human dominance,
Which gives me ten fingers of bone
And a brain to obtain what is mine.
The black ovals upon emerald criss-crossed eyes
Wane with my pain of human complexity.

142 *Distrust*

Cannot trust you,
Though know you well.
Feel your duality,
Dichotomy of love.
Wish you well,
But put my own interests before yours
And well you know it,
So you give back nothing,
And I cannot trust you,
Distancing you through
The picture-frame stage of observation.

143 *The Scapegoat's Cry*

A guilt I feel, which is not needed, yet wanted.
A punishment I know, which I long to suffer.
Their mindless cruelty pleases me though hurtful
And simpers like a friend, wanting to please me
For pain grows pure in nervous self-defence
And soon I start to love the thrill of cruelty,
The bully's bow that fears to face his equals.
I love the lashing wildness of his anger
Which bears me up to face humiliation
I thrill with pain as order, calm and neutral
Returns to numb my ache in recompense.

144　*The Choice*

You saved my life with your rock love.
Steadfast gaze, pillar of ice,
That would not let me sink into the helter-skelter,
But drew me into your own shadow-cave of knowing.
Long ago, it seems, I declined the blackness of giving all
For the yellow butter sunlight, godless laughter,
And when a moment ago I looked into your tranquil eyes,
And saw hazel waters moving, smiling, waiting,
I regretted my refusal.

145 *Display*

The person who knows you well –
The knowledge may be fractional,
But you do not know the fraction –
Cannot be avoided, evaded.
So you must submit to the godlike nod,
That slowly mesmerises,
The subtle lowering of the voice,
That reminds you of your telepathic bondage.
And when you try to camouflage
An x-ray effort shoots out, a green flame
To see behind your ploys,
So you can only accept,
And walk around naked,
Hideous, but unashamed.

146 Questions and Answers

'It is rude,' said Alice, 'to make personal remarks.'
The boy with the deerlike face asks the woman,
'Where do you work?' and shrivels away, as she frowns
Pebble-eyed back. 'Why do you want to know?'
No reason explicable, but the age-old wish
To communicate.
She reads between the lines and pours out
Eye-pools of acid onto his frightened scrutiny.
Across the room a girl laughs between ropes of black hair
And shouts, 'I work in Islington.'

If only I knew the answer, the answer,
If I could crack the mirror into a thousand splinters,
If I could reach through to the other side
Like Alice, but what answer did she find?
A fairytale entertainment.
The image I see is an overlapping duet,
The retina trick of a drunkard on a spree,
The white and the black, the knowing and the searching.
Only a glass, a pure glass, can give the answer,
No dust on the frozen surface,
No silvered gleam to distract from the true reflection.
I will throw a diamond rose through the mirror
Into the black night sky, Through the dust particles
Beyond the magnetic sphere of this constellation
And the splintered petals will tinkle a frozen answer.

147 *The Will*

The essence of goodness,
However multiplex one's faults,
Is to rise above
And in losing selfness to become godlike,
A non-person.
Breath exhaled on a snowy day
Cannot be concealed, but puffs out white clouds,
Ghostly against the damp air.
The pressure of the will will out
And away from a bone-house too small,
Will burst from the shrinking body.

148 *Instant*

When the pain rings true,
Like charnel-fire through the body of a snake,
There is the bliss of waiting
For cessation.

149 *God and Satan*

Satan grew so bright
That he sparked out.
God hangs darkly.
Satan whistled a sibilant hiss,
That pierced through to another world.
God is immobile everywhere.
Satan loves and links
With gold rings in a chain of paper-foil,
That slithers apart.
God clamps even polarities together
In a pressure-hold.
That is what
He is.

150 *Psychology*

We live in the age of psychology,
Where quiet and willpower
Have vanished as true qualities,
And have been reabsorbed into the sea of pathology,
Where love and hate may be controlled by biochemistry,
Where sleep and waking
Are merely different manifestations
Of the ego lulled into various states of awareness,
Where God is a conglomeration
Of all the medieval manuals,
Bound together into one neat conformity,
Where the norm is elevated to an abnormal degree
And the abnorm is compressed into mediocrity.
No , I am not mocking,
Not baiting,
Not hating,
Just stating,
And waiting,
To see what further advances are in the making.

151 *Sanity*

Sanity lies in emotional wholeness.
The maniac's mind may be vital and probing
But his feelings are over-developed, so dangerous
To himself and his neighbours and all the community.
A well-ticking intellect with fickle stability,
He speaks to his visitor open and friendly,
With rational meaning and sensible calmness.
An instant's meandering starts up the curtain
Dividing the insane from the sane majority.
His visitors' eyes blink, glaze and lose contact.
He's labelled and separated, alone and still thinking.

152 The Future

Unlike the gypsy in the tent with a glass ball
And a cup of tea-leaves,
I can never quite believe in the future.
My tent is the present moment,
Which cloaks out all things to come.
Trapped by the moist moment of each breath,
I do not see any shapes on the screen of the coming week,
And so I am bound by a caul of disbelief,
For as the days pass by, the birth-pangs of all new ideas
Stretch my vision until I want to shriek
With the agony of a future
That insists itself, despite my stolid denial.

153 *Evil*

Id,
Evil id,
Burning cantankerous in the fires of the self.
Where do I lie.
That chose to be?
Would sing and love and grow.
Down there
Bubbles black
Clotted blood, that is stirred to hatred.
Roots,
Clump into the night,
Where the soul knows
The one,
To whom it belongs.
Death trap of horned gold,
Leaping a grotesque comedy.
Rise
Out slowly finger above palm above hand
And shriek free.

154 *Turbulence*

Cannot find peace of mind,
Blue sky haven,
In the turbulence of craggy stone-sifted quarry,
Black coals crunching over sparkled flints
Cannot find peace.
Only the rough shifting of not knowing,
The ache of the changing motions of the rocks,
As they churn together this way and that,
Granulated squeaks,
Cannot find peace.

155 *Façade*

She wants to be happy.
Her voice is frosted white lace upon a rose glass,
And when a disturbance arises,
Monstrous spider, black against the window-pane.
She freezes its wiry legs
And watches the mouldy remains,
That rot away far on into the winter.

156 *Current of Belief*

Tired of pure thoughts, crisp, snowflake white,
I switched off the current of belief in God
And waited to see what would happen.
Driven along by my own motor-power,
Curious movements, often wires intermingled,
Spirits of energy bouncing along the ground,
Evolved from my fear and hatred.
Magnet removed, I experienced
A chaos.
Switched on the electricity again,
Crossed wires slip back to normal.
Peace of mind, perhaps, but not quite,
Having once glimpsed behind the fence.

157 Double Glazing

You think you made a precise and unusual discovery,
That everybody has a façade, a double-glazing.
Smash away this outer layer and expose the inner glass.
You behave this way with everybody,
Undiscriminating,
Exposing your unhappiness, your fears.
But I consider this continual vandalism
To be even falser than the double barrier
That preceded it.
Leaves no room for layers to be gradually pared away,
Like the peeling of an onion,
Which makes one cry genuine tears,
Not the coal moan of affectation.

158 *The Line of Memory*

Keats wrote somewhere
That when two old friends meet
After a lapse of seven years,
They will be totally changed in every tissue.
I have seen this happen,
Watched them gaze at each other curiously,
Newly estranged,
But drawn together by the line of memory
They each pull out of their minds an image of the past
And dangle it on a string, smiling bashfully.
I would like to label all these images
And place them in a universal library
For the reference of future generations,
But this can never be.
Meanwhile people will write plays and paint pictures
To rid themselves of the ache of old memories,
Which clutter up their minds, swollen to bursting point.
And in the expulsion a shrinking will take place
And a transfiguration.

159 *Over-Exposure*

Tightening threads break through
The churning heart-tissue.
My slow frown
I see for the first time
The face of the Jamaican girl or woman,
The label is inappropriate as is her race.
Fuzzy down of hair, extended nostrils,
Pushed by invisible rings from ear to ear,
She tries to smile,
Soft lips curiously knowing
The black and the white of every day.
Unblinking wet eyes, that stare into mine.
Encounter unfamiliar,
I turn away.

The cliff-face is white from over-exposure.
It is a free choice
To outstare all that is wrong
And see only the blotted remains
Or to feel with the snails crushed into the cliffside.
When the rocks grow to sand, and the seaweed to slime,
All is broken in the floodwaters,
Even the black and white films,
Spotted from over-exposure
Show skeleton figures bent towards the prison camps

Quick march of flashing teeth as the snakes flow in
Onto semi-corpses.
Everyone is black and white and spotted.
To stare through their smiles
Beyond their knowing
And to share the corpse
That they will one day be
Is a free choice,
A choice that is right
Or to let every exposure grow blind and white.

160 *Rat-Race*

Rat-race,
Squeaks in the running.
Leap over a grey back and a brown back.
Prick up your ears twitching to catch some gossip.
Destroy his reputation, her peace of mind.
Run as far as you can over the dead leaves,
For nothing can survive in this climate.
Knife of wind over the runway,
Gasping for breath,
Tiny pointed teeth peep out of sagging mouth,
Surprise of red blood
Pouring out from beneath the grey fur,
A reminder that it is still alive but not for long,
Squeaks in the bleeding.
Rat-race.

161 *Reflector*

You are a non-person.
You do not have thoughts of your own,
Only echo mine and embroider.
In your eyes, small and deep-set grey,
I see myself reflected, minimised.
You write about me as though I were not a person,
But an image,
To pin inside a compartment of your mind,
Made for the purpose of categorisation,
My eccentricities defined
And gummed down for ever
Onto paper.
A photographic lens that captures
With a trick of light.
Clever gimmicks.
After my life's and I will be immortalised
By your skill.
Favour
That I do nor relish.

162 *Tightrope*

A tightrope of people.
Every word must be weighed and measured.
Be careful how you tread.
Each figure walks stiffly enclosed
In his own tube of ice.
Do not breathe too warmly
Or the coating will melt,
A painful thaw,
To swell and to ache,
Exposing
Collapsible limbs.
The bodies will fall off the tightrope screaming.
Hold in your breath and the rigid figures
Will continue to advance their zombie walk.

163 *Eyes*

Five different faculties have we unknowing.
Only tired eyes,
Hot glass,
Crossed lashes,
Remind us.
Four and a half left, we see the world through a barrier,
Conscious for the first time of our separation
From the space around us.
Individual outline defined by helplessness,
We grope in the dark,
Throbbing eyelids, sore skin, ounce of flesh so valuable
Cannot be denied.
Network of red lines spidery in the white iris,
Pink worms in a jelly of milk,
Opaquely
We try to see.

164 *Success*

Problems, that litter the mind like pebbles on a beach,
Grey, large and shiny.
A Nazi task to carry a bucketful up a hill
And throw them down again.
Unending cascade.
Select a few fossils and weed out a shoalful
Of stones, clink upon the sand.
Only by sifting can we see
The pattern of a past Palaeolithic age,
Losing our integrate
In the determination to survive.

165 Oyster

Silently, as the days pass,
We wait for the scratch, the irritation
From which to nourish our thoughts, poems growing,
Like the pearl inside an oyster, swelling day by day
From the grain of sand within.
Ironically, no happiness is possible, or very rare.
For undisturbed by thought, we find a grotesque vacuum,
And so we wait with perverse logic,
For the pinch, the scratch
And enjoy the septic swelling.

166 *The Smile*

The smile,
A long-remembered habit,
Cannot be changed by practice or artifice.
Forty years in an office, her guarded words, quick coughs
And the smile peeps out
From three years old.
Eight teeth beneath the stretched upper lip.
Almost a rabbit, saved by pearly equality.
Naked to the white airlight
The teeth gleam and disappear
Behind the filing system.

The mother, brown arms, goose-pimples,
Magnolia perfume, wipes the soap-suds off her fingers
And onto her apron.
She smiles into the pram,
Closed lips, her teeth cloaked into oblivion,
Along with her own solitary childhood.

167 *Needlepoint*

Through a forest of taboos and ill-fortune
Love winds its devious path,
To strike a heart with the prick of a needle.
The valve is punctured,
Bubbles over into death,
Black blood, to be reborn
A different person, one skin less,
Open to a multitude
Of new and finer pricks.

168 *Four-Leaved*

People
Cluster like clover in the meadows,
One solitary flower by the fence
And here a four-leaved gem,
Arousing admiration and perplexity;
It stabs at so-called normality.
Boundaries divide people,
A delicate membrane here,
And here a skin, a hide, a barrier,
To break the partitions
Is frowned upon.
Only the four-leaved oddity can indulge, succeed
Unpunished.

169 *Two Cures*

The Stoic
Thickens his skin with oil and will-power
Not to feel.
Fortified
By the precaution that all is pain
He grins hugely.

The poet
Scrapes off the outer surface of his skin,
Bare cellulose.
It bleeds differently every day.
The fun of exploration.
Sometimes the flesh is raw.
He weeps with his wound,
But soon recovers defiantly.

170 *Two Sides*

A phone-call from a woman
Who was my rival twelve years ago,
As we sat in his room side by side on a sofa,
Olive-green silk with faded threads of white.
I noticed the black hairs upon her neck,
Her short neck
Set at anxious angle.
The squeak in her voice,
A restlessness probing but never profound.
She stirred my envy.
I watched gloatingly
As she curved a wrist against her chin,
Ugly
In a false attempt to allure.
Now she is a mother.
I feel ashamed. Her attempt was not false,
Yet neither was my vision incorrect.
Both sides of the triangle are just.
They fall from the apex, which is herself
Onto the hypotenuse of perception,
Reflected in the sight of her lover and myself
Today and yesterday.

171 *Involvement*

Hypocritical
With each change of department,
Faction and political party,
We laugh behind your back,
Your retreating figure harmless,
Black suit shrinking into the distance,
We smile unthinking. Not wise to probe too deep.
Compromise in order to survive.
Only when suddenly you swivel round,
Eyes narrowed to angry slits,
Your mouth open in surprise,
Upper lip curved back in disrespect,
A keyboard of white teeth flashing.
Comes realisation.
Lurching heartbeat.
Guilt.

172 *Divorce*

After all this time
Only a brick wall left.
Your head has banged against it uselessly
All these years.
It has not grown any softer.
No indentations to rest upon,
No mossy patches for the cushioning.
You have tried again and again to reach him.
No shadows left to darken the bricks, crudely pink.
The wall stands bolt upright in the naked sunlight
A barrier between you,
And now you must crawl away into the background,
Acknowledging your mistake.

173 *Widow Spider*

They spoke blunt friendship
And their words murdered each other;
Like a female spider
That devours its mate,
She surveyed the void where he
No longer existed,
But snarled feebly, defeated,
Until the next silence should lasso them
Into a frozen circle.

174 *Sophistication*

Warm, friendly voice,
Cultivated adjustment to individuality,
She talks at ease to everyone,
Caring for none.
Gimmicks, trick gestures, here a raised eyebrow,
There a lifted arm, head turned to the side,
Twitch of cheeks, strained nod,
Eyes understanding.
Blue pupils naked upon the white iris,
Joined to every glance in total comprehension
And complete indifference.

175 *Photo*

Now that you are thirty
You have recaptured the features
Of your childhood, sturdy obstinacy,
Little-boy petulance.
The downcast face to retreat into the corner and sulk.
In the intervening years of adolescence,
When you really grew up,
You were defiant and rebellious, a man upstanding.
But now you have shrunk back into your old shadow,
The hand slipping into the right glove,
A comfortable habit.
I cannot blame you. Perfectly natural to retrieve
The proper image.
But I miss the shiny negative.

176 *Fifty Per Cent*

Can you not accept the fact
That I can only love you fifty per cent?
The remainder is taken up with jealousy.
I am a half and half person,
And I do not wish to change.
So if you want a hundred per cent dotage
Do not come to me.
Or perhaps the others are just as fractional as myself,
But conceal it.
They play tricks on you,
Whereas my duplicity is naked.
Thus in all logic
You must accept my calculated honesty
And love me with whatever degree of fervour
Seems appropriate.

177 *No Resting Place*

Now
No love is here
To you
Rolled back into the black ether,
Your own self
Where you belong.
Long ago
I found a surprise,
Summer growing,
Green upon green,
Touched me.
And ever the humming grows louder,
Where there is no end
To the one creation.
New weeds will grow apace
Yellow furze, brown bushes,
The sickening turning over
Lurches back into Sartoris' opened eye.
There is no resting place,
I want to cry.

178 *Infection*

Infection
Takes us out of the cardboard paint
Into an underworld,
Where the body bubbles black and sick,
Spawning with some knife-stab
To grow whole again.
Bubbles float along the air from the clay pipe,
Red streaks in the soap-silk skin
And the child blowing breath after breath,
Laughing at the slow flow.
Blood and germs mingle and fight within the body
And the owner continues to advance,
Pinned down momentarily
By black bubbles of sickness.

179 *Wasted Years*

The wasted years
Thrown down a well,
Brown tidemarks swoop up high;
Can never be pulled back,
Dwindled to a sixpence of mud,
No frantic retrieval of every split second
Can fill in the white hairs of the empty days,
Before the act of decision clamped down
The expansion into adulthood.

180 *Acquiescence*

I accept this, the stifled past,
I can endure
With my acquiescence.
A tribute to those
Half-skeletons, the cramped angles of their lives.
I can redress the balance,
Annul my debit
To the forgotten surfs and mothers of fourteen
And deeds woven by archival convention;
The love that could never be given
And the strange tumbling down of days
One upon the other
In infantile confusion.

181 *Frost*

The half people,
Who live cramped days
Like tulips
Bitten by frost
Before the air has blown them out.
Will never know
The strange expanse.
Instead they breathe securely
The dead hours.

182 *Meditating*

All digging down to the same roots.
We reach the green
And wait.
Stopped
Upon a patch of cool,
The eye trapped
Into a glazed holding.
Wait here.
Minutes are nothing, not even hours.
We are here, here in the leaf-green grip.
Before and after is dancing,
But now
The static eye blinks, pupil glossy curve of blue
Mesmerised to a marble
Of water.
Deep down
To the point of a pool,
Grey and silver layers
Of probing.

183 *Six Haikus*

Peach row of faces
Frozen into scrutiny,
As words resolve pain.

The cat jumps up in delight
To lick the ice-cream plates,
While we wash up.

Beneath the wooden pier
The slits of sea gleam through,
Blue as April sky.

Around the boardroom table
Sit half a dozen men
In grim discourse.

Beyond the library hush
A piano clinks out chords,
Then fades away.

The silence presses down,
Willing me to speak
Or scream or shout or weep.

184 *Respect for the Elders*

Respect for the elders.
Is it a tyranny of the old over the young,
An ancient hierarchy gone wrong,
Or the growth of wisdom over the years
So that at the point of death
All is conceived in the upturned eye,
Roll of white egg?

The old page of the Bible
Has been torn out and crumpled away
Today,
So that only the jottings are left,
Shepherd on the hillside
Under the burning Middle Eastern sun
And another son bringing home
A smile of obedience
To the old parents still lodged
In his childhood home.

185 *Snowdrop*

I am one person.
Sometimes the snowdrop opens,
Key turns and the petals curve out.
To give
Sun meets the frostbitten fringe of brown tatters.
Only one person.
Stream of thought always alone,
Inside the white bird of head,
Flows out ice-cream clear on smooth days,
To lasso another
Merge
Then falls back into two twines.
One person alone
Has given you the full stream onslaught,
Ice-deep melting waves of lace
Into translucency
And now,
Frozen over by glass-case of winter,
Fall back again into the bird,
One person alone.

186 *The Ascetic*

Will eat
Only the bitter flesh of apple and lemon.
Live on rub of sparkle stones against the knuckles,
Cushions of shingle
To wear away the padded flesh;
Granulated winds will wash me clean.
Tear away the blood luxury
Into knives of bone
Skeleton,
Pearl white,
Purified hollow of cheeks,
Where the shadows reflect the old worn-out trunks
Of passing trees,
That have eaten their way into the ground
With roots of tentacle.

187 *War Baby*

Listening
To the hardy battleaxe
Anecdotal with pride
Behind the beige upholstery,
I changed from audience to participant
And lingered in the spiral of her voice-box,
Where children sobbed a full ten minutes
For their fathers,
Departed with the army;
Until at the last
I was a three-year-old girl
In rubber dungarees,
Playing
Anyhow
But never anywhere
In trouble

188 *Occupational Therapy*

Grey slabs that peel down
To neat shapes
Beneath manipulating fingers.
Soon the patients will leave
With new personalities,
The spare grey slabs discarded,
A gift to the memory of the word,
Just as Adam bestowed a spare rib to Eve
And watched the consequences grow.

189 *Camera*

You hate my barren mind
And long for the round green leaf bush
That trembles to every vibration of the wind
And grows fatter every year.
Yet I can only spread a white silence
That seeps into the world around me
And clarifies the images
Into a photographic portrait for ever.

190 *Sacrifice*

Do not be dependent upon the one
Whom you would wish to lean upon,
But keep yourself free
The black nugget of identity.
A wheel with gold sparks spinning and flashing
Will revolve day by day,
Catching new loves within its circle
And forking away
The old road,
Until one day
Concentrated thought, drops of selfhood,
Will knit you together with the outer world
And you will both be reunited
With the surprised smile of a bonus
That had been willing to be sacrificed.

191 *Fallen Away*

There was the first man
And the first woman
The others fell away
Replicas of the father and the mother,
And the earth began to crumble
When the flowers grew,
Tiny images that sprang up,
New and rubbery into the surprised air.
We are all fallen away
From the dead hanging air,
The hard outline of wood and steel and aluminium
Into the gift of present vision.

192 *Song of the Crow*

Inside my head
Fly
A white bird and a black bird
The white bird unrolls a sheet of lace before my eyes
And sings of peace;
The black bird croaks that I am no better than the rest
To stand one day amidst the rows of bodies,
Dead pillars of white chalk
And share the final writing upon the wall.
The white bird hands me gifts,
Nuggets of gold
And watches the hours fly across.
Swollen into bubbles;
They burst and pass below.
The black bird stares,
Eyes buttoned into tight reproach,
And crows
The living moment.

193 *We Follow Our Gods*

We follow our gods
Doggedly,
Making of them what we will;
Unmaking
Those that bend
And refuse to torment.
Those strange sunglassed hours
When everybody loves
Everybody,
A cavernous insistence
Still beats the humdrum timpani of hatred;
And a whirring of lorry-wheels
As
Back
Down
The well
They grow dumb
Shoe-steps forwards
Will find along the dust
A new flight of dust.

194 *Fire*

You turn your loves into gods,
Pillars to lean upon,
White fire
Along the day
Hover.
These ghosts of strength,
Sad-eyed,
Willing,
But unable to open the eye
Of the window
Which cuts the sky
Into white fire.

Strength of you,
Crag of shoulders,
Wedge of eyes,
Scrutinise.
You spindle a thread,
Straight as the crow flies,
Truthful,
While the silhouettes around you
Sharpen in surprise
And the window
Cuts the sky
Into white fire.

195 *Tulip*

Fixed
Upon a tulip,
I saw
Blue tinged upon pink,
Like lips in winter;
Severe
Drew the centre
Of whirling Saturday
Down,
Compressed
To the growing point.
Where static
Lies the root of
His pain
And mine,
To whirl endlessly,
Mocked by angels upon a pin,
Who enjoy
What they can understand,
Which we shall never know.

196 *Smiled Upon a Face*

Smiled upon a face
That offered nothing in return.
Eyes brown stones.
Caverned into the skeleton,
Where the flesh receded
And grew saggy,
A death's head,
Lumbering down the corridor,
Pulling back to old arches of cloisters
And grey places,
That fizzled into silence
Before they started the coil
Of turbulent vision.

197 *Cycle*

Leaves crush branches,
Emerald sting of spices;
Stones edged with corners press into worms
And splinter the red tongues of jelly.
Sky upon skull upon heel
Weigh down
To this larva cycle of
The spinning earth.
Cannot stop,
Caught up
In the onslaught.
Cruel to crush,
But no schism
Can separate the stones away from the earth;
Bodies that float into a long airshaft
Will fall, decay.
Compressed
Is this wheel,
Spinning,
Cohesive,
To gravity.

Germs,
Yellow grubs,
Beads on a string,

Tell a rosary
Of all the diseases
That grow.
This body is a myth:
Four sausages stuck to a lollipop.
The head grins.
A keyboard of teeth
Play a tune
On the xylophone
Plaintive clink,
Like dripping water,
Knows it will fall
Into a whirlpool
Of decay,
Disintegrate
Beneath the fresh earth.
The soil is good and moist
Enough to thrust up snails and larvae.
Beneath the sky,
Wind blows a sail of sweeping Wedgwood
On a hot day,
Burnt into the blue.
The Earth is quiet enough to hear itself ticking
As it remembers all the bodies it holds
In the grip of love.
Vacantly the sphere
Revolves
In the blink of an eye.

The old man sleeps
In the launderette,
Slumped upon a settee of pure alcohol
He wheezes to catch his breath;
An air bubble, caught somewhere
In the red plantwork of his ventricles,
Emits a thin whistle.
If only the knotted organ would
Swell in and out again,
Like the syncopated glove it used to be,
The washing behind the convex glass
Dangles one way and then the other.
Caught in a hiccup,
It cannot complete the cycle
While the sleeper, bent into the chest
Of his brown raincoat,
Dreams of the earth spinning around on its axis
Until the sky and sea all tumble back
Over the green fields
Through the black pathways
Of the night.

A cycle of futility and decay,
As birds fly, wings flutter downwards,
Turn to grey soot;
Each morning the alarm-clock bell rings in dismay
To find itself trapped again

In that 24-hour game of chance.
And people smile.
Disembodied Cheshire cat grins,
Which stay in the memory
Long after the happy day,
And everything that crumbles
Learns once again to cohere
In that cycle of futility and decay.

Everyone must be broken at the wheel.
Turn around
At the centre of all things,
There lies a beating heart
That signals the rhythm
Between the cracks of the pavements
And the twigs on the branches.
The cars that press along the road
In time to the stamp and grip
Of wheels against the ground
And a fantail of birds that splay across the sky
Grains against the blue,
Swimming helplessly.
The love between us all wheels into hatred
And back to love again
Carelessly,
Yet generous with the easy tumble forwards
Of the pulse
That tells the day and night.

198 *Sun on the Track*

Sun on the track,
Three rods of fire,
Slipping endlessly along the crushed field of stones.
The parallels change,
The bars intersect
Like a film out of sequence.
The journey goes on,
Goes on.

199 *No Further Can I Go*

No further can I go surely
Than to sink
To the centre of the earth,
Where churning lava performs its cycle daily,
Burnt out to ashes.
In that split second,
When metallic sky closes against the ground,
Is a shattering.
Air vibrates and surfaces are frozen into
Bare solidity.

200 *Wallflower*

Out of the barren mind
Flew
A wallflower,
The last to dance
And the first to arise
Into surprised life,
Grew
Flustering and wounded
By the strange winds,
That cut in sharp contradiction
And persisted.
Its cloying perfume
Will endure
Always.

201 *Peace*

Slowly
Unfolds
White salt peace,
Falling
Away from the action of silence
Into my shadow
That layers the floor with dust.
Half good,
Half thinking wind it clings.
The cutting off would be
A death.
I can look this moment straight
And fly to the bull's eye,
All around the circles grow larger and larger
Spreading out into the world
Of traffic and sky and tower-blocks,
Concrete and glass windows.
Tiny figures walking down the streets
Between crevices of buildings.
Here on high, I can watch the ants march by,
Slowly
Unfolds
White salt peace,
Falling
Away from the action of silence
Into my shadow.

Index of Poems

Note: this index includes page numbers for poems published in the companion volumes, The *Dream of Stairs* and *Before and After the Darkness*.
* = this volume.
B = *Before and After the Darkness*
D = *The Dream of Stairs*

Acorn* 113
Acquiescence* 223
Adulthood (B) 47
After the Quarrel (D) 49
Afterwards (D) 184
Age* 103
Ago (D) 144
Aim, The (D) 65
Alien (D) 183
Anchor-man (D) 206
Ants (B) 60
Apple-Blossom Scent (D) 24
Ascetic, The* 229
Aversion* 31
Awakening (D) 171

Bag, The (D) 122
Ballad (D) 73
Ballroom, The (D) 38
Bank Holiday* 85
Beethoven (B) 67
Before and After the Darkness (B) 54
Being (D) 138
Belief (D) 204
Between Before and After (B) 38
Bio-Energetics* 140
Black and White Universe (B) 488
Black Star (D) 170
Blackbird (D) 98
Blind Man, The* 67
Blue (B) 29
Bluffer, The* 49
Boast, The* 59
Bones* 91

Bore, The* 70
Boredom* 95
Brain* 182
Bubble* 62
Bureaucrat, The* 34
Burnt Out by the Shadows (D) 63
Bus* 115

Cactus* 121
Call* 25
Camera* 232
Cave God (D) 208
Chain* 40
Change (D) 91
Chastity D 33
Chawton House (D) 181
Chicken Bone (D) 59
Choice, The* 186
Christmas Eve* 159
Clam (D) 58
Combat (B) 41
Communication in Silence* 41
Concrete Ground (D) 82
Confession (D) 47
Conflict (D) 165
Consolation of Illusion, The (B) 36
Continue (D) 141
Conviction (D) 137
Corn Song (D) 214
Couple, The (D) 45
Corrupt (D) 169
Cotton-Wool Words (D) 55
Cousins (D) 28
Cracked Heart (B) 34

INDEX OF POEMS

Creation (D) 135
Crocodile (B) 72
Crossed Line* 46
Crowd* 65
Current of Belief* 198
Cut-outs D 53
Cycle* 240
Cynic (B) 44

Dance, The (D) 211
Day* 23
Day and Night (B) 68
Deaf Ear, The* 169
Decision (D) 151
Deserted (B) 50
Development (D) 148
Devils (D) 160
Disillusionment (D) 88
Display* 187
Distrust* 184
Divorce* 215
Double Biology* 109
Double Edged (B) 30
Double Glazing* 199
Doubt (D) 167
Downpour* 101
Dragons' Teeth* 80
Dream of Oxford* 158
Dream of Stairs, The (D) 76
Dreams Talk (B) 28
Duality (D) 75
Duel (D) 161
Dust* 42

Earthquake (B) 56
Egg* 179
Enemy, The* 75
Energy (D) 138
Ephraim* 105
Evening Class, The* 133
Evil* 195
Evolution (D) 205
Eyes* 206

Façade* 197
Facets (D) 64
Fainting, The* 154
Fall (B) 31
Fallen Away* 234
Falling (D) 39
False Image (D) 69
Fear (D) 136
Fear of the Lone Self (B) 75
Feathers (D) 120
Fifty Per Cent* 219
Filter* 181
Fire* 237
Fire Song (B) 69
First Love (D) 37
Fishes* 60
Fishing* 93
Flight* 125
Flock of Blackbirds, A* 79
Food-Time* 118
Foretaste* 137
Forwards (D) 191
Four-Leaved* 211
Friday Afternoons* 83
Frightened of the Night (B) 27
Frost* 224
Fulcrum (D) 106
Future, The* 194
Future Nightmare (B) 55

Geometry of the Mind (B) 35
Gift (D) 57
Giving (D) 94
God and Satan* 191
Gold Door (D) 193
Grape Picking (D) 34
Grief (D) 187
Growth* 100
Guilt (B) 40

Hard Road, The (D) 23
Heat (D) 114
Holocaust (D) 164
Honesty (B) 23
Hospital in Winter (D) 86

INDEX OF POEMS

Housewarming (B) 62
Hum of Silence, The (B) 39
Hunger* 117
Hypnosis* 139

*I Wonder What This Constellation Will
  Be* (D) 190
Illusion (D) 124
Image* 132
Incommunicado* 52
Inconsolation (D) 197
Individuation (D) 156
Infatuation (B) 42
Infection* 221
Insect* 165
Insight (D) 200
Instant* 190
Intercom* 37
Interior* 143
Interruption* 84
Interval (D) 130
Involvement* 214
It Will Pass (B) 64

Jealousy* 183
Joke, The* 69
Journey* 24

Keyboard (D) 107
Kibbutz* 71
Killing, The (D) 46
Kite (B) 45
Knowledge (D) 209

Label* 129
Last Respects* 141
Laughter, The (D) 52
Launderette* 43
Lemon* 111
Leucotomy (D) 85
Life Story (D) 26
Line of Memory, The* 200
Living-Room* 57
Lizard (D) 119
Losing, The (D) 104

Loss* 150
Lost Between Stone Basins* 102
Lost (D) 79
Love (D) 134
Luck (B) 25
Lunch (B) 65
Lunchtime* 63

Madwoman, The (D) 95
Malaise* 106
Maternity (D) 146
Meditating* 225
Meditation (D) 74
Meeting* 92
Memories of a Solemn Childhood (B) 66
Memory* 178
Midday (D) 35
Midnight at the Station* 152
Misunderstanding* 88
Moment* 47
Monday Morning* 29
Moon-Treasure (D) 77
Morning Break* 44
Morning* 28
Mouse* 164
Museum Piece* 98

Nail Armour (D) 115
Nature (D) 143
Needlepoint* 210
Neurasthenia (D) 83
Nice Child (D) 27
Night* 149
Nightmare (D) 121
Nine to Five-Thirty* 33
Ningo Pin, The (D) 196
No Danger* 135
No Further Can I Go* 245
No Mother (D) 147
No Resting Place* 220
Nocturne (D) 125
Not to See Him Again (B) 58

Occupational Therapy* 231
Off Peak* 68

251

INDEX OF POEMS

Old Woman* 110
On the Steps* 97
Onion (D) 93
Open Door, The (D) 123
Outsize* 74
Over-Exposure* 201
Oyster* 208

Panorama (D) 168
Paper Children* 39
Parasite* 108
Park-Time* 86
Parting (D) 50
Party Games* 156
Party Time* 155
Passing (D) 62
Passive Involvement* 168
Past, The (B) 21
Peace* 247
Percentage (D) 89
Photo* 218
Pier* 123
Pity* 90
Platform* 153
Poet, The* 172
Poetry (D) 126
Portent* 51
Praise (D) 219
Preserve (D) 202
Preview (D) 29
Primary School (B) 46
Protection (D) 41
Psychology* 192
Pulse (D) 140
Puppet (D) 142

Quarrel, The (D) 48
Question (D) 158
Questions and Answers* 188
Quick Birth (D) 25
Rainy Day in the Tourist Season* 87
Rat-Race* 203
Reading* 48
Reality* 160
Reality Smiles (B) 18

Reclamation (D) 166
Reconciliation (D) 207
Reflector* 204
Regeneration (D) 101
Regret (D) 90
Rejection (D) 51
Release (D) 149
Remember (D) 70
Reminder* 167
Rendezvous, The (D) 36
Respect for the Elders* 227
Restoration (D) 68
Resurgence (D) 192
Return (D) 189
Revelation (D) 81
Rhythm (B) 63
Roaming* 180
Rope (D) 66
Rosanna* 136
Roses (D) 187
Routine* 134

Sacrifice* 233
Salt (B) 52
Sanity* 193
Sartoris* 36
Saturday Afternoon* 114
Saturday Night (B) 26
Save This Soul (D) 195
Scapegoat's Cry, The* 185
Schizophrenia (D) 84
Search, The* 170
Security (D) 210
See-Saw (D) 105
Selfhood (D) 128
Separation (D) 56
Shades (B) 49
Shadows* 89
She Searched for Happiness (D) 182
Shell (D) 133
Shock (D) 185
Shyness* 142
Signs (D) 203
Silence (D) 177
Silk-Worm* 99

252

INDEX OF POEMS

Silver (B) 74
Sin (D) 80
Singer, The (D) 113
Six Haikus* 226
Six o'clock* 124
Skull-Light (D) 127
Smile (D) 44
Smile, The* 209
Smiled upon a Face* 239
Snowdrop* 228
Something Is Lost (B) 24
Song of a Schizophrenic Monk (D) 112
Song of the Crow* 235
Sophistication* 217
Soul, The (D) 198
Spellbound (D) 40
Spider (D) 129
Spiral of Light (D) 60
Spur (D) 163
Squatter, The (B) 61
Stepping Outside* 144
Stifled* 82
Stones, The* 126
Street Dance* 81
Success* 207
Suicide (D) 175
Summer* 61
Summer Evening* 130
Sun on the Track* 244
Surprise* 145

Talents, The (D) 150
Teatime* 96
Telephone* 45
Television* 166
Ten Days of Penitence* 177
Those Who Do Not Question Much* 104
Three Witches (B) 48
Through the Barrier* 38
Through the Needle's Eye (B) 22
Tightrope* 205
Time* 26
Time Frozen (B) 70
Time Machine* 94

Time Suspended (D) 108
Time's Whispering Silence (B) 71
To Create (D) 19
To Forestall* 112
To Grieve (D) 186
To Speak (D) 215
To Write* 173
Topsy-Turvy (B) 32
Torpor* 53
Trafalgar* 73
Tree and Leaf (B) 77
Trendy People* 138
Tryptich (D) 157
Tube* 131
Tube-Time* 32
Tulip* 238
Tunnel (D) 145
Turbulence* 196
Twentieth Century (D) 155
Twins (D) 162
Two Cures* 212
Two o'clock (B) 33
Two Sides* 213

Ugliness* 58
Ugly, The (D) 97

Vacuum* 72
Verdure* 107
View* 122
Vision (D) 103
Vision, The (D) 111

Waiter, The* 119
Waiting, The (D) 116
Waitress, The* 120
Wakening (D) 102
Waking* 27
Wallflower* 246
Wandering Through the Days (D) 61
War Baby* 230
Wasted Years* 222
Water (D) 172
Water-Bird (D) 54
Waves (D) 199

253

INDEX OF POEMS

We Follow Our Gods* 236
Wedding, The (D) 67
Weep Before God (D) 174
Whale (B) 59
Whale Ideas (B) 19
When His Arms Closed Around You (D) 43
When Morning Is Whiter than Shell* 30
When the Door Opens (D) 194
When the Hands Freeze Cold, (D) 78
When You Love Someone So Strangely (D) 42
Why Write?* 171
Widow Spider* 216
Will (B) 37
Will, The* 189
Winter* 151
Winter Dampness (B) 17
Worms* 50
Writing* 174

Yellow Flame (D) 212
Yoga* 163
Yoga Dance (D) 110

Index of First Lines

Note: this index includes page numbers for poems published in the companion volumes, The *Dream of Stairs* and *Inside the Stretch of My Heart*.
* = this volume.
B = *Before and After the Darkness*
D = *The Dream of Stairs*

Line	Poem	Book	Page
A flock of blackbirds / They cry and cry	*A Flock of Blackbirds*	*	79
A frightening thing is memory	*Memory*	*	178
A glass of water and a tube of	*Suicide*	D	175
A gratuitous gift / A letter of good fortune	*Luck*	B	25
A guilt I feel, which is not needed, yet	*The Scapegoat's Cry*	*	185
A hidden chunk / Vulnerable / When	*Reality*	*	160
A jade silk-worm in the gallery	*Silk-Worm*	*	99
A man and a woman in a restaurant	*The Joke*	*	69
A phone-call from a woman / Who was	*Two Sides*	*	213
A poem cannot be contrived wilfully	*To Create*	D	19
A ring of friends, arms linked softly	*The Dance*	D	211
A shy polythene bag / Keeps the washing	*Shyness*	*	142
A swarm of birds fly fanlike overhead	*Panorama*	D	168
A tightrope of people / Every word must	*Tightrope*	*	205
A typewriter tapping, dust upon my desk	*Morning Break*	*	44
A wide expanse of gleaming spirals	*The Dream of Stairs*	D	76
After a long gap between poem / And poem	*Writing*	*	174
After all this time / Only a brick wall left	*Divorce*	*	215
After the broad road, / White as a pillar	*Dragons' Teeth*	*	80
After the cinema / The painted eyes and	*Christmas Eve*	*	159
After the quarrel / We sat in the night-	*After the Quarrel*	D	49
After the visitors departed / Slowly from	*Yoga*	*	163
All digging down to the same roots	*Meditating*	*	225
All that summer / The trees cracked	*First Love*	D	37
An all-devouring void inside me bleats	*Hunger*	*	117
Anchor-man, / Black as the night you are	*Anchor-man*	D	206
Apple-blossom scent, / Sickly strong	*Apple-Blossom Scent*	D	24
At certain times of the day / The time of	*The Stones*	*	126
At one o'clock, / Head swollen to a	*Bubble*	*	62
At the back of the moon, / Beyond the	*Moon-Treasure*	D	77
At the bottom of my mind's cave	*Cave God*	D	208
At the end of the long day / When the	*Remember*	D	70
At this moment, / I have curved round	*Moment*	*	47
At three o'clock / The line that cuts the	*Roses*	D	187
Baby breathing, mother peeping	*Development*	D	148
Bank holiday Monday white afternoon	*Interruption*	*	84
Bare carpet peeling off / Soft fluff	*The Squatter*	B	61
Beyond the footlights of the open-air	*Summer Evening*	*	130

INDEX OF FIRST LINES

First line	Title		Page
Birds singing silver / Outside rain-	*Sartoris*	*	36
Black star / Make me strong / Against	*Black Star*	D	170
Blighted / Earth waved return to its	*Fall*	B	31
Blue aproned lady waddles to and fro	*Teatime*	*	96
Blue cushions / Plumped out	*Living-Room*	*	57
Books dust / Woolly paper at edges	*Tree and Leaf*	B	69
Bonds that break and merge / Day in	*Chain*	*	40
Born to a bellow of music outside the	*Life Story*	D	26
Bought on an impulse, / It cost three days	*The Bag*	D	122
Brown and pink arms / And faces	*Crowd*	*	65
Can it ever be recovered, / Integrity of	*Restoration*	D	68
Can never give enough, / As much as I	*Giving*	D	94
Can you not accept the fact / That I can	*Fifty Per Cent*	*	219
Canniballed / Not aware	*The Past*	B	21
Cannot feel a proper sorrow, / Cannot	*To Grieve*	D	186
Cannot find peace of mind, / Blue sky	*Turbulence*	*	196
Cannot live glad hours all the time	*The Open Door*	D	123
Cannot trust you, / Though know you well	*Distrust*	*	184
Cats spawn kittens. / Sun ties cellophane	*Growth*	*	100
Changed. / The white skin was still the	*Meeting*	*	92
Charcoal drawings / Fading into fibres	*Museum Piece*	*	98
Circle / Shoes in the morning	*The Bureaucrat*	*	34
Cold clatter of feet against the pavement	*Concrete Ground*	D	82
Cold feet on an office afternoon	*Boredom*	*	95
Cotton-wool words, / Cloud-spun	*Cotton-Wool Words*	D	55
Cousins / Are siblings once removed	*Cousins*	D	28
Crack / Between dawn and morning	*Something Is Lost*	B	24
Cricklewood in dust, / Garbage gleaming	*Saturday Afternoon*	*	114
Crisp voice, newly ironed / Along with	*Memories of a*	B	66
Crossing the road / I though I recognised	*False Image*	D	69
Curiosity infinite / There is much work	*Yellow Flame*	D	212
Curiously / Relieved I stare at the knife	*Six o'clock*	*	124
Cut out with regret, / Pull back into	*Regret*	D	90
Daily routine of / Coil upon coil of	*Nine to Five-Thirty*	*	33
Despair, the whale / Swallow up the	*Whale*	B	59
Discovered / Sucking slowly on a straw	*Midday*	D	35
Do not be dependent upon the one	*Sacrifice*	*	233
Down sticks of rain, / Neck gasping fish	*Downpour*	*	101
Each day month week / We polish shoes	*Rhythm*	B	63
Each one of us / Will one day be broken	*Forwards*	D	191
Endless book of days / Each night	*Journey*	*	24
Ephraim in his bedsitter / Smooths out	*Ephraim*	*	105
Every day / Springs forth twins	*Energy*	D	138
Every time I fall in love / Sharpness of	*Infatuation*	B	42
Everyone must bear between their fingers	*When the Hands...*	D	78
Fallen away / From the old God-love-	*Being*	D	138
Falling short / Compromise / As the air	*Between Before and*	B	38
Fear of motherhood. / A broken glass	*No Mother*	D	147
Five different faculties have we unknowing	*Eyes*	*	206
Fixed / Upon a tulip / I saw / Blue tinged	*Tulip*	*	238
Flames and torture-rack of a Tudor epic	*Stepping Outside*	*	144

INDEX OF FIRST LINES

Fools / That grin and have faith	Those Who Do Not	*	104
For four years we have worked in the	Communication in	*	41
Force open these eyelids shuttered so	Waking	*	27
Four girls / Sharing gossip / At lunchtime	Lunch	B	65
Frost and fog through the windows	View	*	122
Frozen fingernails turning yellow	Blackbird	D	98
Gilted leaves / That paint the sun	Guilt	B	40
God / Spreads his / Warmth and peace	Praise	D	219
Grey slaps that peel down / To neat shapes	Occupational Therapy	*	231
Hair aflame with the heat, / Eyes	The Reading	*	48
Hatred dwells among people, / Like	Verdure	*	107
He mocked her drawing, / Black criss-	The Killing	D	46
Heart cracked into jagged edges / Like	Cracked Heart	B	34
Heat dissolves me, frees the barriers	Heat	D	114
Her head is cider-swollen to a bubble	No Danger	*	135
Her voice hit the air with a subtle sweep	The Singer	D	113
Hidden in a telephone kiosk / On an	Last Respects	*	141
Hideous jollity / Kipper on the table and	Adulthood	B	47
High above the earth / Upon a tightrope	Rope	D	66
His anger murdered her with eagle eyes	Bones	*	91
His eyes / Black / Will hypnotise	Geometry of the M.	B	35
His moccasins spattered with green mud	The Rendezvous	D	36
His poised / Eyes, / Leaping fish	Fishing	*	93
His writing is more real to him than life.	To Write	*	173
Hot silence / Divides the air / Into good	The Hum of Silence	B	39
Hypocritical / With each change of	Involvement	*	214
I accept this, the stifled past / I can endure	Acquiescence	*	223
I am a child of the twentieth century	Twentieth Century	D	155
I am a puppet, / Jerking one and two and	Puppet	D	142
I am a shell / Catching echoes of the past	Shell	D	133
I am a turnip gone mouldy / And my top	Corrupt	D	169
I am an egg. / A black band in the middle	Egg	*	179
I am frightened of the night / That suckers	Frightened of the N.	B	27
I am one person /Sometimes the snowdrop	Snowdrop	*	228
I am pale and white / Calm and quiet	Chastity	D	33
I can never know you completely	Kite	B	45
I could tear you out of me,	Chicken Bone	D	59
I do not know / Whether I have the	Surprise	*	145
I dreamt I had a tiny ear growing inside my	Future Nightmare	B	55
I felt myself falling through a hole in the	Return	D	189
I have forgotten it, / The guilt which lay	The Losing	D	104
I have known you in another life	Shadows	*	89
I have nothing, / Unless I have all	Spur	D	163
I have peeled off the façade	Onion	D	93
I have scrubbed the house from top to	Disillusionment	D	88
I have wilfully flicked an ounce of flesh	Rejection	D	51
I hear an inner thump and must express	Individuation	D	156
I hear time's whispering silence in my ears	Time's Whispering	B	71
I hung upon the splintering beam of oak	Fire Song	B	69
I know a man / Who goes to church	Crocodile	B	71
I lay on the garden hammock / Stared up	Conviction	D	137

INDEX OF FIRST LINES

First Line	Title		Page
I sang a song of yearning and derision	Corn Song	D	214
I see you shadow-bound / Between the	Shades	B	49
I thought of you, picking grapes	The Bore	*	70
I thought she was so cool, so untouchable	Trendy People	*	138
I wish, I wait. I wait and I wish.	Ballad	D	73
I wonder what this constellation will be	I Wonder What This	D	190
I wrote away at ease until the poets	Why Write?	*	171
Id, / Evil id, / Burning cantankerous in	Evil	*	195
Ideas / Like ants / Multiply, swarm and	Ants	B	60
If I could sink down into my stomach	Fulcrum	D	106
If we never see each other again,	Parting	D	50
If you could love the person / Whom you	Combat	B	41
I'll give you a ningo pin, / A pin of God	The Ningo Pin	D	196
In a café by a window / There is no	Vacuum	*	72
In another life / Many transmigrations	Lizard	D	119
In Chawton House, the birthplace of	Chawton House	D	181
In France / The mistletoe sprouts on oak	Parasite	*	108
In me / You stay / White fire	Through the Needle's	B	22
In the antique shop on the corner	Torpor	*	53
In the falling away, / Grey wings of bird	Sin	D	80
In the peak of the rush-hour / The man	Off Peak	*	68
In the tube / At twenty minutes to nine	Tube-Time	*	32
In this Victorian parlour / Eggshell walls	Interior	*	143
Infection / Takes us out of the cardboard	Infection	*	221
Inside my head / Fly / A white bird and	Song of the Crow	*	235
Invisible strings / Sweep the squares	Paper Children	*	39
Is it a nightmare or a dream? / I see	Dream of Oxford	*	158
Is this an eternal waking / After the eye	Afterwards	D	184
It does not lie in a house and home	Security	D	210
'It is rude,' said Alice, 'to make personal	Questions and	*	188
Keats wrote somewhere / That when	The Line of Memory	*	200
Knowing how he does not love you	Spiral of Light	D	60
Leap into the white void of Monday	Monday Morning	*	29
Leaves crush branches, / Emerald sting	Cycle	*	240
Let the ugly speak / In angular smiles	The Ugly	D	97
Life is not symmetrical, / A layer of	See-Saw	D	105
Lilting and loving, loving and lilting	The Ballroom	D	38
Lime teeth, / Straw of grass	Kibbutz	*	71
Listening / To the hardy battleaxe	War Baby	*	230
Listening to two conversations at once	Crossed Line	*	46
Lost between stone basins / And lions	Lost Between Stone	*	102
Love, once wanted, / Panacea to blunt	Double Edged	B	30
May / Peace birds trees sway / Welcome	It Will Pass	B	64
Midnight at the station / Shadows	Midnight at the	*	152
Midnight in my square bedsitter	Nocturne	D	125
Morning wakening, / The chalk-white	Wakening	D	102
Mother breaks through / The barriers	Time	*	26
My heart like frozen seaweed hangs	Love	D	134
Nature often belies living experience	Nature	D	143
Net curtains quiver / Like loops of jelly	Two o'clock	B	33
No better than the next / We rise and fall	Routine	*	134

INDEX OF FIRST LINES

No further can I go surely / Than to sink	*No Further Can I Go*	*	245
No moment will ever be more real than	*Through the Barrier*	*	38
No one / Can wipe out the fear that is	*Fear*	D	136
No one knows, / Where all the energy	*Preserve*	D	202
No security is possible, gateway to your	*Gift*	D	57
Not to see him again / Never the eyes	*Not to See Him*	B	58
Now / No love is here / To you / Rolled	*No Resting Place*	*	220
Now that the pendulum has swung	*Time Suspended*	D	108
Now that you are thirty / You have	*Photo*	*	218
Oh black and white machine of information	*Television*	*	166
On a primrose day in March	*Lemon*	*	111
On a windy morning in October	*Primary School*	B	46
On each shoulder is perched an object	*Duality*	D	75
On the corner of the arcade / Between	*Grief*	D	187
On the boat pub / Pretentious / Sea curls	*Night*	*	149
On this afternoon, / Tranquil gold	*Maternity*	D	146
One man was there / I loved / Face black	*Black and White U.*	B	43
One soul was lost. / It went tumbling	*Tunnel*	D	145
Only God knows the truth / Of the	*Knowledge*	D	209
Our friendship came to nothing, petered	*Burnt Out by ...*	D	63
Our love, fulfilled, would not be so	*Separation*	D	56
Out of the barren mind / Flew	*Wallflower*	*	246
Over the hills / Olive-black trees and	*Lost*	D	79
Over the morning / Hangs	*Portent*	*	51
Pain produces logic / To anaesthetise	*Roaming*	*	180
Parabola of water. / Hoop bent	*Water-Bird*	D	54
Party games are fun. / Let's throw away	*Party Games*	*	156
Pass on to the next / It grows	*Continue*	D	141
Pause, / While London changes	*Trafalgar*	*	73
Peach row of faces / Frozen into scrutiny	*Six Haikus*	*	226
People/Cluster like clover in the meadows	*Four-Leaved*	*	211
Perhaps this daily journal, / Pages of red	*The Search*	*	170
Pity / Passes through the layered	*Pity*	*	90
Please believe / That I want nothing	*Facets*	D	64
Potted plant between the lace of curtains	*Cactus*	*	121
Problems/That litter the mind like pebbles	*Success*	*	207
Rat-race, / Squeaks in the running	*Rat-Race*	*	203
Reality painful / As gasping fish out of	*Quick Birth*	D	25
Reality smiles, / Does not grow any	*Reality Smiles*	B	18
Red telephone kiosk / Leaning against	*Time Machine*	*	94
Respect for the elders, / Is it a tyranny	*Respect for the Elders*	*	227
Rosanna is silent and blonde and haughty	*Rosanna*	*	136
Rush-hour malaise. / Slow plodding of	*The Blind Man*	*	67
Sanity lies in emotional wholeness	*Sanity*	*	193
Satan grew so bright/That he sparked out	*God and Satan*	*	191
Saturday night / The broken down fire	*Saturday Night*	B	26
Save this soul / Catch its dropping	*Save This Soul*	D	195
Scorching light of day / White fire	*Morning*	*	28
Scrawny blue-veined hand still clutching	*Old Woman*	*	110
Sharpen the brain / To a fine point of	*Brain*	*	182
She laughed. 'I looked out of the window	*Twins*	D	162

INDEX OF FIRST LINES

She searched for happiness / As if it were	*She Searched for*	D	182
She slept in a chair by the table	*Dreams Talk*	B	28
She speaks glibly of intellectual despair	*Cynic*	B	44
She wants to be happy. / Her voice is	*Façade*	*	197
Silently, as the days pass, / We wait for	*Oyster*	*	208
Sitting at twin tables / I see	*Fishes*	*	60
Sleep in wonder. / Do not know where	*Interval*	D	130
Slowly the evil / Has seeped into my soul	*The Ten Days of*	*	177
Slowly the sweet-sour juice trickling	*Grape Picking*	D	34
Slowly / Unfolds / White salt peace	*Peace*	*	247
Smile upon us, lazy beauty, / Out of	*The Vision*	D	111
Smiled upon a face / That offered nothing	*Smiled upon a Face*	*	239
So I survived and compromised with	*Regeneration*	D	101
So many gaps, / White patches, which	*Percentage*	D	89
So many things given / Mornings that	*Deserted*	B	50
Some eagle hovers overhead	*Call*	*	25
Something / Of Hell / I saw / With this	*Foretaste*	*	137
Standing in the black rain	*Passing*	D	62
Stay attuned to the forces of life	*Pulse*	D	140
Strange to see this familiar face	*Dust*	*	42
Strength of you / Crag of shouldera	*Honesty*	B	23
Stretched out in a darkened room	*Vision*	D	103
Sun on the track / Three rods of fire	*Sun on the Track*	*	244
Sunday afternoon. / Out of the glass-	*Park-Time*	*	86
Sunday afternoon, / White as salt	*Salt*	B	52
Sunday television, an Italian wartime	*Reminder*	*	167
Sunflayed, / Cross-kneed upon steps	*On the Steps*	*	97
Take a petal, imprint it on your mind	*Meditation*	D	74
Taken by surprise / I squirm	*Food-Time*	*	118
Ten years ago they sat together at a	*The Wedding*	D	67
Tepid afternoon tea-leaf tea / Fills	*Stifled*	*	82
The birds wing jerkily across the mauve	*Flight*	*	125
The black days, / Metallic white sky	*The Waiting*	D	116
The boast / Spilled out of my lips	*The Boast*	*	59
The book of my mind lies open	*Schizophrenia*	D	84
The broken-down fire / Fuses the flat	*Ago*	D	144
The bus is swamped with raincoats	*Bus*	*	115
The cat, a seething kettle, / Paws and	*Aversion*	*	31
The challenge of an enemy	*The Enemy*	*	75
The coach is flashing through the hills	*Misunderstanding*	*	88
The consolation of illusion / Love and	*Consolation of I.*	B	36
The crazy sect are dancing / Along	*Street Dance*	*	81
The criminal is ill, / Steals in surprise	*Topsy-Turvy*	B	32
The daddy long legs / Cannot scuttle	*Insect*	*	165
The day I put away the tranquillisers	*Awakening*	D	171
The day skips across the murmuring sea	*Day and Night*	B	68
The death of someone you love	*Inconsolation*	D	197
The earth turns rebel against itself	*Day*	*	23
The empty spaces and wasted days	*Resurgence*	D	192
The essence of goodness / However	*The Will*	*	189
The falling in love down through a hole	*Falling*	D	39

INDEX OF FIRST LINES

The fat shopper in the fitting-room	*Outsize*	*	74
The first time I glimpsed Hell	*Preview*	D	29
The girl in purple trousers lay on the	*Release*	D	149
The girl sways her pregnant hips	*Earthquake*	B	56
The girl with the operated nose	*Change*	D	91
The God in my head is more real	*Skull-Light*	D	127
The green eyes of the black tomcat	*Jealousy*	*	183
The half people / Who live cramped days	*Frost*	*	224
The human soul floats down from	*The Soul*	D	198
The laughter grew / Into gold coils	*The Laughter*	D	52
The Man on the Cross, He rose	*Question*	D	158
The mouse / A tiny grey ball of fur	*Mouse*	*	164
The park on Easter Monday	*Bank Holiday*	*	85
The party was a slit of light under the door	*Party Time*	*	155
The person who knows you well	*Display*	*	187
The pigeon coos mercilessly / Outside	*Intercom*	*	37
The poet looks out / Of his head / Sieves	*The Poet*	*	172
The pounding Beethoven, / Beats	*The Deaf Ear*	*	169
The railway line of life / Never to be	*To Forestall*	*	112
The silence has been broken / By a string	*The Evening Class*	*	133
The smile, / A long-remembered habit	*The Smile*	*	209
The snow is falling February white	*Hospital in Winter*	D	86
The soul searcher / Lays aside his pen	*Conflict*	D	165
The spirit entered them; / Sat smoking	*Insight*	D	200
The Stoic / Thickens his skin with oil	*Two Cures*	*	212
The telephone / Black furry ear	*Telephone*	*	45
The torn fingernail, which you will pull	*Nail Armour*	D	115
The Tube on a Saturday evening	*Tube*	*	131
The washing-machine's stomach	*Launderette*	*	43
The wasted years / Thrown down a well	*Wasted Years*	*	222
The waves roll in / Day after day	*Waves*	D	199
The will frittered out / Would not obey	*Will*	B	37
There are signs, / Strange to interpret	*Signs*	D	203
There is a gold door in the sky	*Gold Door* D	193	
There is a madwoman gaunt and brown	*The Madwoman*	D	95
There is a test-card C of selfhood	*Keyboard*	D	107
'There is an answer to every problem	*Holocaust*	D	164
There is no cure for being one person	*Selfhood*	D	128
There was the first man / And the first	*Fallen Away*	*	234
They are mocking the devils within me	*Doubt*	D	167
They cut a slice out of the brain,	*Leucotomy*	D	85
They didn't mean to quarrel.	*The Quarrel*	D	48
They scrub the drawers / And sweep	*Housewarming*	B	62
They spoke blunt friendship / And their	*Widow Spider*	*	216
Things are not so easy for you now, my love	*Before and After*	B	54
Thinking is away from the grain	*Blue*	B	29
Thirst. / A crystal glass ball of ice-cold	*Water*	D	172
This death / I cannot quite believe in	*Shock*	D	185
This dismembered leg / From an ancient	*Age*	*	103
This hypnotist / Has a sandalwood voice	*Spellbound*	D	40
This park greenery / Overwhelms	*Fear of the Lone Self*	B	67

INDEX OF FIRST LINES

First line	Title		Page
This passage along the days, / Does it	Evolution	D	205
This restaurant is like a fore-echo	The Waiter	*	119
Three words. / Brief answer to his	Incommunicado	*	52
Through a forest of taboos and ill-fortune	Needlepoint	*	210
Through bleary lattice-work of rain	Rainy Day in the	*	87
Through the railings, / Beyond the rail-	Platform	*	153
Thursday afternoons are for double	Double Biology	*	109
Tightening threads break through	Over-Exposure	*	201
Time frozen into ice-drops / Clings	Time Frozen	B	70
Tired of pure thoughts, crisp, snowflake	Current of Belief	*	198
To be loved / Is to stop thinking	Protection	D	41
To hear sometimes the grey groan of	Tryptich	D	157
To pay back in energy / The gift I have	The Talents	D	150
To run into a long tunnel, blackness	Poetry	D	126
To wake up from a three o'clock	Nightmare	D	121
Today, / Floating on an eiderdown of	Feathers	D	120
Try to absorb / The news on television	Passive Involvement	*	168
Twin pawns of ivory on a chessboard	Duel	D	161
Two decades and a half have passed	Creation	D	135
Uncorrupted, He participated, / Tore off	Reconciliation	D	207
Unlike the gypsy in the tent with a glass	The Future	*	194
Untidy Friday afternoons, / Ends of	Friday Afternoons	*	83
Virginia saw it too, / The door	Neurasthenia	D	83
Walking away from the doctor's	Malaise	*	106
Walking between the great stone	Image	*	132
Walking one by one / Down the white	Lunchtime	*	63
Walking over the grass on an evening in	Label	*	129
Walking, windswept / Over the slatted	Pier	*	123
Wallflowers scorching blood in July	Summer	*	61
Wandering through the days	Wandering ...	D	61
Warm, friendly voice, / Cultivated	Sophistication	*	217
We follow our gods / Doggedly	We Follow Our Gods	*	236
We lay in a circle on the carpet, heads	Hypnosis	*	139
We live in the age of psychology	Psychology	*	192
We met on a blistering summer's	Ugliness	*	58
We sat in the damp evening air	Confession	D	47
We were talking in a hut on a strange	The Bluffer	*	49
Weep before God / When the ice breaks	Weep Before God	D	174
Whale ideas / Blubber home	Whale Ideas	B	19
What is the use of this strained sensibility	Song of a...	D	112
When all the love has dwindled away	Acorn	*	113
When his arms closed around you	When His Arms...	D	43
When I tore away the curtain of my	Revelation	D	81
When I was a child, a naughty child	Nice Child	D	27
When I was fifteen, / I stood in front of	Devils	D	160
When I was young and the rain poured	Worms	*	50
When it is cold and empty, / Black sky	Belief	D	204
When morning is whiter than shell	When Morning Is	*	30
When my anger broods and stirs	Three Witches	B	48
When the dog ran away in the middle of	Loss	*	150
When the door opens, / The silence will	When the Door	D	194

INDEX OF FIRST LINES

When the pain comes / Gold spots upon	*The Fainting*	*	154
When the pain rings true, / Like charnel	*Instant*	*	190
When we met, / Cardboard figures	*Cut-outs*	D	53
When you love someone so strangely	*When You Love...*	D	42
Where the will lies / Flicker to the right	*Decision*	D	151
White dots in the air / That fizzle	*Silence*	D	177
Who loves the grey tent of darkness	*Winter*	*	151
'Why do you smile all the time'	*Smile*	D	44
Why, when I look at silver, / Can I not see	*Silver*	B	66
Will eat / Only the bitter flesh of apple	*Ascetic, The*	*	229
Winter dampness is a fungus	*Winter Dampness*	B	17
Wish to be reclaimed by the Spirit	*Reclamation*	D	166
Without the selectivity / Of a brain filter	*Filter*	*	181
Yoga dance, / Fly away to the north and	*Yoga Dance*	D	110
You are a non-person. / You do not have	*Reflector*	*	204
You are a spider flashing out silks,	*Spider*	D	129
You can try / For a minute, for an hour	*The Aim*	D	65
You hate my barren mind / And long for	*Camera*	*	232
You have chosen the hard road	*The Hard Road*	D	23
You know I feel for you, / Your every	*Clam*	D	58
You lay above me cutting off the blue	*The Couple*	D	45
You saved my life with your rock love	*The Choice*	*	186
You say everything so explicitly	*To Speak*	D	215
You teach me how to plumb the depths	*Beethoven*	B	67
You think you made a precise and unusual	*Double Glazing*	*	199
You turn your loves into gods / Pillars	*Fire*	*	237
You, who dwell in a cold and Nordic	*Alien*	D	183
You work long, steaming days here	*The Waitress*	*	120
You would like me better / If the grey	*Illusion*	D	124
Zany clown, / Red velvet jeans stretching	*Bio-Energetics*	*	140

www.ingramcontent.com/pod-product-compliance
Lightning Source LLC
Chambersburg PA
CBHW032041090426
42744CB00004B/78